THE ART OF WAR
FOR EXECUTIVES

The
ART OF WAR
for EXECUTIVES

DONALD G. KRAUSE

A Perigee Book

THE BERKLEY PUBLISHING GROUP
Published by the Penguin Group
Penguin Group (USA) Inc.
375 Hudson Street, New York, New York 10014, USA
Penguin Group (Canada), 10 Alcorn Avenue, Toronto, Ontario M4V 3B2, Canada
(a division of Pearson Penguin Canada Inc.)
Penguin Books Ltd., 80 Strand, London WC2R 0RL, England
Penguin Group Ireland, 25 St. Stephen's Green, Dublin 2, Ireland (a division of Penguin Books Ltd.)
Penguin Group (Australia), 250 Camberwell Road, Camberwell, Victoria 3124, Australia
(a division of Pearson Australia Group Pty. Ltd.)
Penguin Books India Pvt. Ltd., 11 Community Centre, Panchsheel Park, New Delhi–110 017, India
Penguin Group (NZ), cnr. Airborne and Rosedale Roads, Albany, Auckland 1310, New Zealand
(a division of Pearson New Zealand Ltd.)
Penguin Books (South Africa) (Pty.) Ltd., 24 Sturdee Avenue, Rosebank, Johannesburg 2196,
South Africa
Penguin Books Ltd., Registered Offices: 80 Strand, London WC2R 0RL, England

ISBN: 0-399-53150-5
PRINTING HISTORY
First Perigee edition / February 1995
Revised Perigee trade paperback edition / April 2005

PERIGEE is a registered trademark of Penguin Group (USA) Inc.
The "P" design is a trademark belonging to Penguin Group (USA) Inc.

The Library of Congress has cataloged the original Perigee edition as:

Krause, Donald G.
   The art of war for executives / Donald G. Krause. —1st ed.
      p. cm.
   "A Perigee book."
   ISBN 0-399-51902-5 (pbk. : alk. paper)
   1. Management. 2. Leadership. 3. Success in business. 4. Sun-tzu, 6th cent. B.C. Sun-tzu ping fa.
I. Title
HD38.K688   1995
658.4—dc20   94-29606
                                                                              CIP

PRINTED IN THE UNITED STATES OF AMERICA

10 9 8 7 6 5 4 3 2 1

To Susan Ruth Bradshaw, Rebecca Anne Krause,
and Elizabeth Lorraine Krause

ACKNOWLEDGMENTS

I would like to thank Dr. Bob Shively of the Babcock Graduate School of Management, Wake Forest University, for his assistance over the years, but particularly for supporting this book during its critical early stages. Bob has been associated with the Babcock School, as a professor of organizational behavior and as dean, for over twenty years. He is due a large part of the credit for the school's fine program and glowing national reputation.

I would also like to thank Dr. Chang Miao, principal of the West Suburban Chinese Language School in Villa Park, IL. Dr. Miao translated the original Chinese text that formed the basis for my interpretation. Dr. Miao has also given me the kind of insight into the Chinese culture and character that can only come from a person who was born and educated in China.

INTRODUCTION

Sun Tzu is a semi-mythical figure, more than likely a combination of several people, perhaps a father and son or grandson (Sun Pin), who lived in China about 2,500 years ago, around the time of Confucius. Drawing on experience gained while leading successful military campaigns, Sun Tzu developed and handed down a collection of concise and immensely useful concepts governing the art of warfare. These concepts evolved into a written document during what is called the Period of Warring States (403–221 BCE). The great Chinese warlord Cao Cao cited Sun Tzu's concepts as the source of his success in consolidating China into one country. Cao Cao transcribed Sun Tzu's ideas into a short book, *The Art of War*, which has been the blueprint for waging war and doing business in China and the Far East ever since.

In the latter half of the twentieth century, *The Art of War* became a worldwide management phenomenon. Un-

derstanding and using Sun Tzu's principles is now a require-
ment for everyone who wants to succeed in business any-
where in the world. But getting to the essence of the
material can be difficult. While *The Art of War* is a short
book, only thirteen chapters, the original material reads
more like notes written down during a series of lectures or
informal discussions over an extended period of time. Chap-
ter titles do not always convey the ideas covered in a given
section. Furthermore, unrelated ideas are thrown together
and related ideas are discussed in separate sections. For those
willing to work through *The Art of War*, however, Sun Tzu
presents a coherent set of effective principles that, once mas-
tered, can be used to create a powerful competitive advantage in almost every phase of business and life.

Mastering *The Art of War* with Sun Tzu's Principles

For the business executive, mastering *The Art of War* involves integrating Sun Tzu's principles into all personal and
professional affairs on a day-by-day, moment-by-moment
basis. Mastering *The Art of War* involves considering every
business situation, indeed *every* situation, in light of its potential for conflict and its opportunities for profit. This does
not mean becoming belligerent, argumentative, or merce-
nary (unless it is useful to do so). In fact, just the opposite;
a calm, objective, reserved approach will serve much better.
But mastery does mean automatically assessing the
strengths and weaknesses of people encountered, friend
and foe alike. It does mean paying constant attention to developing character and sharpening leadership skills. It does
mean carefully considering other people's words and ac-

tions to uncover their true meaning and significance, not just taking them at face value. At the bottom line, however, mastery of these principles is worth the effort. Mastering Sun Tzu's principles means that when an opportunity does appear, the raw material of competitive advantage will be readily available.

Sun Tzu presents two levels of principles in *The Art of War*. The two levels can be termed **strategic** principles and **tactical** principles. Strategic principles are those applied on a constant, consistent basis, regardless of the situation. They are designed to provide the foundation and framework for successful competitive operations. There are three strategic principles: *Commitment*, *Observation*, and *Preparation*. Without appropriate application and integration of the three strategic principles, overall competitive success will never happen.

Tactical principles are those applied in direct response to a specific opportunity or threat. There are six tactical principles: *Assessment*, *Adaptation*, *Leverage*, *Deception*, *Timing*, and *Pace*. Each tactical principle is like a strand of fiber making up a strong rope. By itself, a given strand may break under heavy strain or intense pressure; but by weaving the strands together, one is able to create a rope that will handle any load.

In addition to the two types of principles, Sun Tzu employs three aspects, or points of view, in discussing the application of his principles. These aspects are: the individual, the individual's working group, and the competition. When applying Sun Tzu's principles, it is necessary to evaluate the situation from all three aspects to understand the scope and effect of a given approach or method. The three aspects are, of course, not mutually exclusive. They are three subjective versions of the same objective reality; the same situation observed from three separate but intimately related perspectives. The ability to conceptualize a situation from each of the three points of view is a fundamental skill.

Strategic Principles

Commitment is the first strategic principle. On an individual and working-group level, commitment and character set the stage for eventual victory. Without commitment, nothing happens. Sun Tzu says, "In general, serious competitive engagements will succeed only if people are wholly committed to plans and goals. When people are committed, they act with unified purpose. When they have unified purpose, no defender can stop them, no attacker overcome them. The nature of people is to ardently strive to reach any goal to which they are committed. Put your organization into a situation where they have no choice but to commit to your goals and they will succeed beyond their imagined limits."

The drive and desire to succeed in difficult situations derives from the depth of character. The nature of a person's character is a combination of personality, ideals, and commitment. Character is shaped over a long period of time. Furthermore, character has no moral dimension; it is an objective reality. The morality of a person's character is determined by his actions. Think carefully about the force of character. It will determine the emphasis and direction of a person's actions. Sun Tzu teaches, "Know your enemy and know yourself." If a person's character is known, his motivation will also be known. This provides a significant competitive advantage.

Executives exhibit personal character through leadership style. Leadership style and personal character are two sides of the same coin; leadership style is the external manifestation of internal principles. Particular combinations of character traits fit certain situations better than others. When a person with a suitable combination of character traits is able to fulfill the leadership needs of a specific group or constituency, he will find himself in a position of leadership, providing he has taken the time to develop basic leadership skills. This is how terribly flawed people become powerful leaders. They shape their character to fit the needs of a specific constituency. Recent political and business events, indeed events throughout history, have shown the necessity for evaluating the character of leaders before thrusting them into positions of power over people's lives and fortunes.

On a group level, Sun Tzu emphasizes character as a critical element of preparation. Putting effective people into positions of authority is absolutely necessary to create an organization that can successfully execute adaptive strategies during competitive engagements. Select subordinates carefully, then test them thoroughly. Give them the time and opportunity to fail in situations where the consequences are not dire.

Character flaws create opportunities for competitive advantage. Sun Tzu teaches this about using the character flaws of others against them: "Utilize the character flaws of your opponents in order to defeat them. Look for these five traits: If an opponent is reckless, we can cause him to waste his resources. If an opponent is timid, we can seize his resources. If an opponent is short-tempered, we can cause him to be rash. If an opponent is self-important, we can deceive him with flattery. If an opponent is overly concerned about loss of position or reputation, he will hesitate before making a difficult decision at a critical moment. These character flaws greatly restrict an executive's potential success. They are the cause of loss in competitive engagements. These character flaws cause executives to fail and companies to die. Eliminate them in yourself."

Observation is the second strategic principle. Develop the habit of watching people and situations closely, even when you are not threatened or under stress. Watching closely provides raw data about what is really happening. Be alert for indications that things are not quite what they seem. But learn to observe dispassionately, without evaluation or judgment. Evaluation and judgment are appropriate for taking action, when action is determined to be necessary. During periods of watching and waiting, judgment and evaluation may in fact be a great weakness.

Here is why: One of the easiest and most commonly used competitive strategies is what might be termed "intentional confusion." Intentional confusion is the strategy of moving in circles without any apparent direction. Sun Tzu says, "Amidst the chaos of organizational politics or the competitive marketplace, the skilled executive is able to detect patterns in the activities of his rivals. He, on the other hand, carefully disguises his own objectives. He moves resources around in seemingly random ways, almost as if he is wandering in circles. He appears confused and arbitrary, but he cannot be defeated. This kind of apparent disorder can only be the outcome of expert organization and precise communication. The illusion of fear and confusion can only come from great courage. Seeming weakness is a function of realized strength."

This strategy works particularly well because people tend to disregard the details of situations they have become accustomed to over time. Experienced leaders use this tactic frequently. One way to defeat intentional confusion is to be constantly aware (without becoming paranoid) that people are creating illusions in order to hide their true intentions. When they are ready to act, they will vary their activity pattern slightly, something will be out of place. An observant person will notice the small change if he has not already made a judgment to disregard another person's seemingly trivial, totally pointless, or just plain annoying activities. People are seldom able to launch an attack without first giving some indication of their intent.

Subordinates should be trained to report observed facts and situations without leaving out details that they think the leader may not want to hear and without inserting opinion in place of fact. Sun Tzu says, "Accurate intelligence is the foundation of profitable operations. When an executive fails, it is often due to reliance on folk wisdom. Folk wisdom is that body of unchallenged and generally incorrect assumptions perpetuated by those who lack real knowledge and information. Folk wisdom exists at every level of every organization. Rapid, profitable adaptation feeds on facts, not unsupported assumptions."

Observation is a two-way street. Competitors are watching, too. As Napoleon Bonaparte put it, "Everywhere I go, I am watched by a thousand pair of eyes." This can be used to create an advantage. Sun Tzu says, "Succeeding in a direct engagement on a competitor depends on deceiving him. If your stratagems are obvious to your competitor, no matter how good they are, he can defeat them. Concentrate on your objective, but develop your strategy in secret. Keep your competitor off-balance by constantly changing form. In this way, your methods are hidden. You are free to move as fiercely as a winter storm or as gently as a summer breeze. You can attack like a roaring fire. You can stand firm like an unshakeable mountain. You can strike like lightning, a searing bolt of force from the darkness piercing to the heart of your opponent's weakness. Confuse your opponent's focus and you will be able to harvest his constituency. Cause him to lose his direction and you will conquer."

Preparation is the third strategic principle. Effective execution on a tactical level, that is, at the point in time when opportunity presents itself, depends on preparation long before the moment of action arrives. Preparation includes developing organizational structure, streamlining processes, positioning resources, encouraging flexibility, and training personnel.

Organizational structure is fundamental to successful execution. Sun Tzu says, "Structure is the way activity is organized and managed. Structure is considered separately from leadership, because leadership must function within structure. Structure includes how your activities are financed; how well you and your employees are developed and trained; how your organization creates and evolves products and services; how well technology is employed; how flexible or inflexible, responsive or unresponsive, effective or ineffective, are your policies and procedures. Structure shapes the basic capabilities of individuals within an organization. Structure defines the primary interface with external business factors and determines how easy or difficult it is to enter and dominate a market." Many of the specific suggestions Sun Tzu gives about organizational structure are, of course, archaic. But the idea that structure must fit purpose is still valid.

Process can help or hinder execution. Sun Tzu warns executives about inappropriately focused process: "An executive misuses power when he focuses too much attention on process rather than progress. When procedure-minded executives attempt to control activities with cumbersome rules, they choke operations and hamper profit. Aggressiveness—balanced by reason, flexibility, and imagination—fuels the kind of adaptive evolution and rapid execution that promotes success."

Resources required to complete competitive operations should be on hand before beginning operations. When discussing causes of executive failure, Sun Tzu points out, "If all other things are equal, and an executive orders a poorly equipped, poorly supplied, poorly trained, poorly organized, or poorly funded group to challenge another group that is adequate in these areas, the cause of failure is lack of resources. No amount of courage or determination can make up for lack of critical resources."

Flexibility in structure and flexibility in attitude is essential to executing competitive operations. Sun Tzu says, "Only an executive who is flexible enough to adapt his strategy to changes in competitive circumstances can effectively manage resources during competitive operations. An executive who is not flexible enough to adapt his strategy to changes in circumstances, even if he has wide knowledge of people and methods, will not be able to take advantage of this knowledge. An executive who is not flexible enough to adapt his strategy to changes in circumstances, even if he recognizes an advantageous opportunity, will not be able to assign the right person to take the right action at the right time."

Training personnel engaged in competitive operations is essential to success. Sun Tzu says, "Treat your employees well; train them thoroughly. The success of the organization is built on the individual success of its members. If you lack relevant training or proper equipment, your engagement will be defeated. When managing people, if you criticize an individual before he feels loyalty to you, he will not obey your orders in the future. Further, once you have established a bond with an individual, if discipline is not enforced, he will not follow orders, either. Without obedience, it is hard to employ people effectively. Therefore, if you direct your employees through an appropriate organizational structure and maintain control through appropriate discipline, your people will be competent. If you train and motivate your employees with clear expectations, they can be relied on in critical situations. If you train and motivate your group with vague expectations, they will fail you. When expectations are clear and organizational structure is appropriate for the task, people trust their leaders and submit to control." Training provides the foundation for obedience and control in competitive situations.

Several of Sun Tzu's commentators have added notes to the text about the importance of training for competitive engagements. One of the earliest and best known of these commentators was Wu Chi (also known as Wu Tzu). In roughly 400 BCE (about a century after *The Art of War* was first composed as a written document), Wu Chi wrote: "When men die in war, it is usually because they get themselves into trouble through ignorance. Therefore, the first order of business is to train and instruct them. Start with one man. He can then instruct ten other men, who can instruct one hundred, who can instruct one thousand, until the entire army is instructed. [Notice the similarity to Six Sigma training methodology.] In training, drill your troops to form circles from squares without tripping over themselves, and to sit down and stand up in unison. March them from left to right, and forward and back. Divide them up and concentrate them again; unite them and disperse them. When they can do all this without confusion, give them weapons and begin combat training. The short men carry spears and axes; the tall men carry bows and crossbows. The strong carry flags and banners; the brave carry bells and drums (for communications). The weak serve food and move supplies. The wise make plans. Train men of similar backgrounds together for mutual support and encouragement. Practice communications and signals. At one drum beat, order arms. At two beats, form ranks. At three beats, eat rations. At four beats, prepare for action. At five beats, march forward. Unfurl the banners only after hearing drum beats and listening to orders."

Communication among group members during a competitive engagement is critical. Effective communication under stress depends upon training and preparation beforehand. Sun Tzu says, "Direct engagements and other critical situations generate intense emotions. In circumstances where emotions run high, rational thinking may suffer. Further, clear communication among members of your group may be blocked. For these reasons, during intense situations use devices that will minimize distraction and reduce chaos by refocusing attention on objectives. If your employees are unified by clear communication during critical moments, those who are bold will not attempt unwise initiatives and those who are timid will not ignore opportunity or shrink from the fray. This is the way people are managed during crises. Remember, however, that your messages and signals to each other might be intercepted by your competitors. Therefore, confuse your opponents by mixing false signals with real ones. But fooling your opponents requires a high level of discipline and commitment among members of your group." Attaining a reliable level of communication competence under difficult conditions requires careful practice.

As Sun Tzu says, "The executive who prepares carefully before entering into competition understands how to leverage strength. With well-considered preparations, one can develop alternatives for action that offer the greatest opportunities for promotion and profit. With adaptive execution, one can turn these opportunities into ultimate victory."

Tactical Principles

When the need for action arises because of a perceived opportunity or threat, Sun Tzu recommends employing a combination of six tactical principles. These principles are: *Assessment, Adaptation, Leverage, Deception, Timing,* and *Pace.* These principles can be woven together to form a strong, yet flexible, approach to winning in competition.

Sun Tzu covers *assessment* of the competition and competitive conditions from several different angles: assessing relative strength and weakness, assessing the competitive terrain, assessing deployment of competitive resources, and assessing a competitor's strategy.

Assessing relative strengths and weaknesses is a fundamental principle of strategic planning, in Sun Tzu's time and now. Sun Tzu recommends, "When considering competitive strategy, assess your plans and gather information using the following questions: Which executives create an atmosphere of genuine cooperation among employees and associates? Which organization fosters enthusiasm among its customers, managers, employees, suppliers, shareholders, creditors, regulators, and other stakeholders? Which executives have developed leadership character according to sound principles? Which actions are favored by national, local, and intramural political agendas? Which ideas are consistent with current economic conditions? What type of structure is better able to take advantage of key factors in the marketplace? Which executives are better trained? Which organization has more knowledgeable directors, executives, employees, customers, and suppliers? Which executives build people? Which organization truly rewards merit and encourages personal growth?

"Find the answers to these questions. They will predict which plan has the greatest chance of success. The executive who heeds this advice is sure to succeed. Such a person should be placed in an important position. The executive who disregards this advice will fail. Such a person should be dismissed. Taking into account the elements of competitive analysis discussed above, each executive is charged with creating plans for competitive action that leverage personal and organizational strength and minimize weakness. By competitive actions, I mean activities that bring an individual or an organization into conflict with other individuals or organizations. Leveraging strengths gives you a competitive advantage. Competitive advantage is the key to promotion and profit."

Competitive terrain assessment means analyzing the situation in terms of how difficult it might be to reach targeted constituencies. Sun Tzu structures analysis in terms of six competitive situations. He says, "We can describe six competitive situations as accessible, ensnaring, inconclusive, restricted, difficult, and speculative. If all competitors can reach a given constituency or market easily, then the situation is accessible. When the situation is accessible, try to establish a strong position first, this will give you an advantage.

"If it is easy for either side to enter into a competitive engagement, but once involved, difficult to withdraw, then the situation is ensnaring. Under these conditions, when your competitor is unprepared, you can challenge him. Remember, however, that once you are involved, your investment may become excessive, and you may not be able to withdraw without significant additional cost. Therefore, if your competitor is already positioned, it may be advantageous to avoid him. If you cannot get there first, look for an easier target.

"If both sides have difficulty entering and leaving a competitive situation, then neither side may be able to win. The situation is inconclusive. Do not challenge a competitor when you are not confident of winning, even if he is weak. It is a waste of resources. Instead, make your competitor waste *his* resources by allowing him easy access to unprofitable markets or unresponsive constituencies. Wait for another opportunity.

"Restricted markets are difficult to access. Stringent technological requirements, professional knowledge, financial demands, or the like present significant barriers to entry. If you are able to enter a restricted market first, build even stronger barriers, technological, economic, and legislative if possible. In this position, you have the advantage and can afford to await your competitor's challenge. If your competitor has already strongly established his position in this area, he has a significant advantage. Do not engage him unless he has left an opening.

"Where both sides are facing a difficult situation and cannot readily access a market or constituency, if you are able to make inroads first, set up a strong defensive position and wait for your competitor to advance. If your competitor has already established a position, try to make it unprofitable by getting him to waste money defending it. But do not move in too quickly if he begins to retreat. This may be a ploy.

"Speculative competitive situations involve important or profitable constituents who are unknown or remote. These situations are problematic for all parties because they require taking risks whose costs and consequences are largely unclear. In a speculative situation, it is usually difficult to understand what is needed to ensure victory. Therefore, it is generally not advantageous to advance.

"These are the principles for assessing the six different types of competitive situations. When an executive begins to move resources toward an objective, he must carefully examine his campaign in light of these principles."

Assessing competitive deployment seeks to determine the flexibility and effectiveness of assets committed to competitive operations. Sun Tzu says, "Proper application of the principles of offensive strategy requires analysis of the competitive situation. The competitive situation determines what type of adaptation is necessary in order to win. The competitive situation determines whether we should attack or defend, how we can best employ our resources, and what route to take. There are nine different competitive situations. These situations must be examined carefully.

"When a competitor challenges our position before we can concentrate our resources to defend it, we are in a *scattered situation*. If we are beginning to advance into a competitor's territory but have expended few resources in the process, we are in an *uncommitted situation*. In a *scattered situation*, avoid a fight. Concentrate your resources to multiply their power. Keep the competition at bay until you are prepared. In an *uncommitted situation*, match the outflow of resources with expected benefits of success to maintain competitive flexibility.

"If we have established a profitable position in a market that is also profitably occupied by our competitor, we are in a *conflict situation*. If we can advance and retreat easily but it is also easy for our competition to advance and retreat, we are in an *accessible situation*. In a *conflict situation*, do not advance into a competitor's strength. Instead, approach from the blind side; create some kind of advantage before expending resources. In an *accessible situation*, keep your guard up. You can be attacked from any direction. Plan your defenses carefully.

"If the position we occupy overlaps several constituencies and allows us to tap into the different markets represented by these constituencies, we are in an *intersecting situation*. When we have penetrated deeply into another's territory and have expended large amounts of resources to do so, we are in a *critical situation*. In an *intersecting situation*, consolidate your resources. Focus on overlapping market areas to achieve penetration into multiple constituencies. In a *critical situation*, take important positions first. Make sure your technical, financial, and organizational resources are adequate to hold them.

"When we must overcome technical, financial, or organizational difficulties before proceeding, or there are major barriers to reaching the constituents we want, we are in a *blocked situation*. When we continue to commit resources to influence constituents and cannot withdraw without sustaining a loss but several competitors have already been successful in eroding our market position, we are in a *surrounded situation*. When we can survive only if we challenge competitors and win a quick victory but will perish if we delay or are defeated, we are in a *deadly situation*. In a *blocked situation*, break out quickly. Focus on weak points in obstacles and punch through them. In a *surrounded situation*, hinder your competitor's ability to maneuver by limiting access to your position and constituents. At the same time, execute a strategy to break out of the trap. In a *deadly situation*, face the fact that you may not survive. Advance quickly; expend your resources trying to win through and escape. The alternative is a slow but sure death."

Assessing a competitor's strategy requires close observation of his activities and attitudes during the competitive engagement. Sun Tzu says, "Before entering an engagement, study your competitor closely. Consider these things: If your competitor is ready to attack but remains still, it is likely he has some critical advantage to rely on—look for it. If your competitor seems unprepared for conflict but still challenges you, he wants you to advance, leaving behind your defensive positions. There is a hidden agenda here. Investigate it thoroughly. If there is unexplained activity in the market or agitation among members of your constituency, your competitor may be moving behind a screen or using surrogates. When your competitor springs traps and creates obstacles, he is trying to confuse you. If ordinarily supportive constituents suddenly distance themselves from you, your competitor has organized a secret attack.

"Watch for signs from your competitor's group. If there is a great deal of erratic activity, he may be preparing to move quickly. If the activity level is steady and organized, he is making careful preparations. Look for patterns of activity that predict where he is focusing attention.

"If your competitor's communications sound self-effacing but he is still confident, he is preparing to advance. If your competitor's communications are evasive but aggressive in tone, he is preparing to withdraw. If your competitor prepares a generous offer for you to consider, he may be playing for time. Similarly, if your competitor suddenly, and without any apparent reason, offers peace negotiations, he is plotting.

"If your competitor deploys his resources aggressively, he is expecting an engagement fairly soon. If your competitor feints an advance and then retreats, he is trying to lure you into making a response.

"If your competitor uses trickery or subterfuge to sustain his power, he is dealing with a critical threat. If you allow your competitor an obvious opening but he fails to advance, he is tired or weak. If your competitor wanders aimlessly, he is uncertain. If your competitor speaks loudly, he is afraid. If your competitor's group is in turmoil, his leadership is not effective. If your competitor's communications channels are in disarray, his response to a crisis will be chaotic. If your competitor's representatives are short-tempered, they are under emotional stress. When your competitor uses his last available reserves to challenge you, he is desperate. When your competitor's people whisper among themselves in clandestine groups, your competitor is losing their loyalty. When your competitor hands out too many rewards, he has lost the ability to motivate his people. When your competitor hands out too many punishments, he has lost control of his people. When your competitor publicly criticizes his staff, he is not very smart. When a competitor confronts you as if prepared to attack but neither advances forward nor retreats backward, you must study the situation carefully. Search for the important factors you have overlooked."

Adaptation is the primary weapon for winning competitive business engagements. Count Von Moltke, German Army Chief of Staff and military theorist, said, "Predetermined plans can only be effective until the first contact with the enemy. After that, one must adapt." The executive with the greatest capacity to change and flow in response to actual conditions presented during an engagement has the best chance to win. The ability to adapt is grounded in the effective application of the three strategic principles—*Commitment*, *Observation*, and *Preparation*—discussed above.

Sun Tzu recommends using a combination of expected and unexpected tactics (here the word *tactics* refers to specific maneuvers during an actual engagement): "In competitive situations, one normally begins the battle using expected tactics so the enemy's response can be assessed. Certain victory, however, is achieved by using unexpected tactics—that is, by rapidly adapting offensive and defensive actions in response to emerging opportunities. The executive who is skillful at using unexpected tactics has infinite resources. For him, moving from expected tactics to unexpected tactics and back again flows smoothly, like the surface of a great river. The expected and the unexpected begin and end again, like the waxing and waning of the moon. They cycle from beginning to end, like the four seasons, each in its appointed time.

"There are only five notes in the musical scale; but in a lifetime, we could not hear their infinite combinations. There are only five colors in an artist's palette; but in a lifetime, we could not see their infinite combinations. There are only five flavors in cooking; but in a lifetime, we could not taste their infinite combinations

"The evolution of competitive activities gives rise to opportunities to use both expected and unexpected tactics. We could not in a lifetime exploit all the possibilities provided by crafting tactics based on weaving the expected with the unexpected. Expected and unexpected tactics evolve from each other during the ebb and flow of conflict, like a circle with no starting point. Your opponent cannot tell where one begins and the other ends."

Sun Tzu compares the way a successful executive adapts his strategies to the way that water behaves: "Successful strategies flow like water; they adapt themselves to the circumstances of the conflict. When water flows, it avoids the high ground and seeks the low. Successful strategies likewise avoid the enemy's strength and find his weakness. Just as the flow of water adapts to the contour of the land, the flow of victory adapts to the actions of the opponent. Just as water assumes the shape of any container holding it, the tactics of victory must assume the shape of the present situation.

"By observing nature, we see continuous variation and cycles of change. Nothing remains the same in every situation. Nor is one aspect of nature superior to another in every circumstance. Each of the four seasons appears in turn and each has its advantages. Some days are longer and some days are shorter. The moon waxes and wanes. In the same way, the skilled executive crafts his victory by adapting his plans and resources to the place and time of the encounter. He matches his strength against his opponent's weakness. His victory is called a stroke of genius."

Leverage means exercising control over how and when the competition is able to maneuver. Control allows an executive to move the competition into positions where they can be defeated with certainty. Sun Tzu says, "A skilled executive moves his competition; he does not allow them to move him. A skilled executive lures his competitor into advancing by creating the illusion of false advantage; he discourages his competitor from attacking by erecting fake barriers. Hence, his competitor advances toward failure and retreats from success. A skilled executive keeps his rivals on the move and in the dark. If a competitor becomes comfortable, he creates difficulty. If a competitor is satisfied, he creates a problem. If a competitor is calm, he creates chaos.

"A skilled executive appears suddenly, where the competition must rush to defend against him. He occupies places where the competition least expects to find him. A skilled executive positions his resources with ease because he begins his campaign by occupying territory not contested by others.

"If an executive controls the time and place of an encounter, he can make careful preparations and minimize the risk of failure. If one does not control the time and place of battle, no matter how many resources are thrown into the conflict, preparations will be inadequate and failure will occur. According to my way of thinking, if I control the situation, how can a competitor use his resources effectively, even if they are greatly superior? So it is said: with control, victory can be crafted by those with skill. Even if the enemy is strong, with control, I can make him lose his will to fight."

Leverage also means applying overwhelming strength against relative weakness. Sun Tzu continues, "A skilled executive's offensive actions always succeed because he attacks points that cannot be defended. A skilled executive's defensive positions never fail because he defends points that cannot be attacked. Against such an offensive, the competition cannot know where to defend. Against such a defense, the competition cannot know where to attack. The best strategies are subtle—they have no discernable form. The best strategies are obscured—they cannot be penetrated. When formless and impenetrable, one controls a competitor's destiny. When a skilled executive pressures his opponent, he concentrates on weak points and cannot be stopped. When a skilled executive changes position, he moves swiftly and cannot be deterred."

Deception is essential to gaining competitive advantage. Deception magnifies the impact of well-executed plans. Any strategy or maneuver, no matter how clever or sophisticated, can be deterred or defeated if the competition is able to anticipate its use and prepare a reaction. Sun Tzu says, "Succeeding in a direct engagement on a competitor depends on deceiving him. If your stratagems are obvious to your competitor, no matter how good they are, he can defeat them. Concentrate on your objective but develop your strategy in secret. Keep your competitor off-balance by constantly changing form."

Deception hinders an opponent from effective preparation. It also can create a sense of panic and reduce morale among members of the competitor's team. Sun Tzu continues, "Executing successful operations involves shaping circumstances so they are favorable to your strengths and minimize your weakness. Initially, pretend that you are going along with your opponent's tactics. Make your competitor believe you can be led in the direction he has determined for you. Lull him to sleep. In this way, you can execute your carefully developed maneuvers behind a curtain of deception and surprise. From the moment a competitive engagement begins, maintain strict discipline. Communicate only what needs to be known. Act promptly when authorized to proceed. When your competitor shows his vulnerability, adapt swiftly to take advantage of it. Seize the initiative. Turn the tables. Make him dance in time to your music. Evolve your strategy according to the opportunities presented by your competition. Put yourself in position to gain a decisive advantage. So, begin competitive activities quietly and secretly. When your competitor exposes his weakness, move quickly. In this way, your competitor will not be able to adapt in time. The victory will be yours."

Appropriate *timing* of competitive activities will allow an executive to achieve the greatest gain from carefully planned and managed engagements. Sun Tzu says, "Taking on a strong competitor is the same as taking on a weak competitor. It is a matter of creating favorable opportunities and using the power of timing. If your goal is to gain an advantage, then timing is critical. When rushing water carries huge boulders, it is because of overwhelming power. But when the diving falcon breaks the neck of its prey, it is because of precise timing. For the skilled executive, opportunity reveals the target and timing is the trigger that unleashes the power to conquer. The skilled executive creates opportunity by putting intense pressure on his competitor. When his competitor stumbles, he times his attack to produce unfailing victory.

"Effective executives position themselves and their products in situations where they will survive. Then they wait for the opportunity to attack. Survival depends on one's own actions; victory depends on using opportunity provided by the actions of others. Therefore, while an effective executive can always survive, he may not necessarily be able to triumph. Thus, it is said: The path of victory may be marked, but one must walk it carefully. Survival depends on a careful defense; victory results from seizing the initiative at the right moment. If your resources are not adequate to win, take a defensive approach. When the moment is right, move swiftly."

Sun Tzu gives the following advice about the relationship between timing and understanding the competition: "In deciding what time to begin my actions, I use the following guidelines: If I know my group has the resources to succeed, but I do not know whether my competitor is vulnerable, then my chances of victory are half at this point. If I know my competitor is vulnerable, but I do not know if my group has the resources to succeed, my chances of victory are half. If I know my competitor is vulnerable and I know my group has the resources to succeed, but I do not know if the competitive situation allows me to win, my chances of victory are also half. Hence, those executives who experience success advance only when they know the time is right; as a result, they have no need to retreat. Know your opponent and know yourself—you will not lose. Know the competitive situation and the constituents involved also; then your success will be complete."

Pace is the rate at which competitive activities are executed. Pace must be harmonized with the competitive situation in order to achieve success. Sun Tzu reminds the executive to move swiftly enough to achieve objectives but slowly enough to maintain control: "The aim of competitive action should be to realize profit as quickly as possible. If profit is delayed, enthusiasm fades and resources drain away. If activities are continued for a long time without positive results, strength of will and determination to win become exhausted. If unprofitable competitive actions are prolonged, even a large quantity of resources will not be sufficient. When commitment is dulled by loss, when enthusiasm has faded and resources are drained away, competitors will take advantage of your weakness. Overtaken by defeat, no executive, however wise, can prevent decline of his career and loss of opportunity.

"Competitive actions should, however, proceed at a timely pace. Hastily performed operations tend to invite mistakes. But operations that waste time are never profitable. A successful competitive operation need not be complicated. To maximize profit, do simple things well, and do them at the appropriate time. Strategies that cause mistakes or exhaust resources never produce a profit.

"Executives who cannot balance risk with opportunity do not profit in a swiftly changing, uncertain market environment. Accurate information, well-considered plans, and timely execution are the keys. Only those who are comfortable with the pitfalls and ambiguities of rapid adaptation can profitably manage products and services in slippery market conditions. Only those who appreciate and use the knowledge gained from quick and inexpensive experiments and tests can achieve lasting success. Remember, rapid execution of an effective plan is the key. If you move slowly, your competitor will escape and whatever opportunity you had will be lost. On the other hand, do not fragment your organization or fail to provide important resources to advance in the name of speed. If you skip over necessary preparation and move hastily into a difficult engagement, even if you work day and night, you will have little chance of success. Your efforts will be scattered. Your resources will be wasted. Your motivation will be destroyed."

Mastering Sun Tzu's three strategic principles (*Commitment, Observation*, and *Preparation*) and six tactical principles (*Assessment, Adaptation, Leverage, Deception, Timing*, and *Pace*) gives an executive a powerful set of tools that can be employed in every phase of business. Sun Tzu might summarize his principles in this way:

"Effective executives win victories that seem easy to those observing the action. Effective executives are people of normal ability. They do not possess exceptional wisdom or unrelenting courage. Rather, effective executives win because they make no mistakes. They are unfailingly competent. Every action they take, every tactic they employ, contributes to their eventual triumph. By waiting for others to provide the opportunity, they are always in a position to win. Effective executives establish positions where they can survive. Then, they miss no chance to exploit opportunities provided by their market or competition. A winning executive understands the conditions of victory before taking action. A losing executive takes action before knowing *how* to win. Once in a strong position, an effective executive cultivates his own leadership character and develops a responsive organization. In this way, he controls those factors that are crucial to success.

"The skilled executive maneuvers his opponents. He creates favorable opportunities by luring his competitors into vulnerable positions with the promise of easy gains. Then, he waits, patiently and silently, with overwhelming power derived from combining the expected with the unexpected, the obvious and the disguised, for the moment of victory.

"Understanding the competitive situation can be of great advantage to a skilled executive. A skilled executive understands his constituents, his opponent, himself, and the realities all parties face, and thereby he controls victory. He correctly estimates the difficulty of alternate strategies and calculates the resources required. He accurately assesses those factors that require his attention immediately and those that can be dealt with later. He knows the strengths, weaknesses, and capacities of the people involved in the situation—both his own and those loyal to his opponent. A skilled executive wins because he takes the time to know all these things and applies his knowledge to take advantage of opportunities presented."

Organization of Text

The traditional format of Sun Tzu's *The Art of War* contains thirteen chapters. This text retains the thirteen-chapter format. Each subsection of the original text has been numbered to facilitate cross-referencing to literal translations of the material. In addition, the text includes selected passages from a literal translation of *The Art of War*. These passages allow the reader to get a flavor for the language and idiom contained in the original material. Taken together, the business interpretation and the selected literal passages provide the reader with an opportunity to understand, appreciate, and apply the timeless wisdom of Sun Tzu in today's business world.

Estimates

Sun Tzu said:
War is the most important aspect in the survival of the nation. It is the way of existence and nonexistence. It cannot be studied too much.

Therefore, we estimate using five principles and calculate our strategies. Then, we judge our course of action. Of the five principles, the first is called *Tao* (way); the second is called *Tien* (heaven); the third is called *Dee* (earth); the fourth is called *Gian* (leadership); and the fifth is called *Far* (law).

Conquerors estimate in their temple before the war begins. They consider everything. The defeated also estimate before the war, but they do not consider everything. Estimating completely creates victory. Estimating incompletely causes failure. When we look at it from this point of view, it is obvious who will win the war.

I

PLANNING

I-1
Competition is a matter of vital importance to the executive. Competition determines who advances and who retreats, who succeeds and who fails, who profits and who loses, who lives and who dies. The true battlefield of business is in the minds of those whom you serve, that is, your constituents. Every executive has both direct and indirect constituents. Your leaders, your employees, your peers, and your personal clients are direct constituents. Your company's customers, suppliers, and shareholders are indirect constituents. The cumulative impact of competitive actions increases or decreases your power and influence over your constituents. It is therefore essential that competitive actions be carefully planned and properly executed.

I-2
Analyze your plans for action using the five elements of competition. Assess and compare yourself to your opponents to determine the best course of action. Consider everything.

I-3
The five elements are: substance, climate, structure, leadership, and information.

I-4
Substance deals with the essence, purpose, and image of an individual. Substance determines how your constituents react to you, your company, and your products and services. Substance determines whether constituents believe they are in harmony with your goals and objectives. Substance is the foundation of trust. When constituents trust you, they willingly follow your lead. They buy your products. They help you achieve your goals. Once gained, trust forms a strong foundation for advancement. Nurture it above all else. Lost trust brings swift defeat.

I-5
Climate refers to the impact of economic conditions, political agendas, and cultural trends on the competitive situation. To be effective, competitive actions must be appropriate for the existing climate.

I-6
Structure is the way activity is organized and managed. Structure is considered separately from leadership, because leadership must function within structure. Structure includes how your activities are financed; how well you and your employees are developed and trained; how your organization creates and

evolves products and services; how well technology is employed; how flexible or inflexible, responsive or unresponsive, effective or ineffective, your policies and procedures are. Structure shapes the basic capabilities of individuals within an organization. Structure defines the primary interface with external business factors and determines how easy or difficult it is to enter and dominate a market.

I-7

Leadership comes from within. Individual leadership is grounded in character. Character can be assessed in terms of seven factors: self-image, purpose, accomplishment, responsibility, knowledge, loyalty, and example. Organizational leadership is an aggregate of the character and ability of key executives. The effectiveness of organizational activities, and indeed its very substance, depends on the tone and quality of the character of its leaders.

I-8

Information means getting facts—timely, accurate, and meaningful facts—about the reality of conditions and circumstances in the competitive situation. Nothing in competition is more important than fact!

Information also means controlling perception. Perception can be either fact or fiction, depending on the competitive situation. Effective control of perception encourages your competitors and constituents to do what you want them to do.

I-9

Every executive has heard of these five elements. Those who master them will win; those who do not will lose.

I-10

When considering competitive strategy, assess your plans and gather information using the following questions.

I-11

Which executives create an atmosphere of genuine cooperation among employees and associates? Which organization fosters enthusiasm among its customers, managers, employees, suppliers, shareholders, creditors, regulators, and other stakeholders? Which executives have developed leadership character according to sound principles? Which actions are favored by national, local, and intramural political agendas? Which ideas are consistent with current economic conditions? What type of structure is better able to take advantage of key factors in the marketplace?

I-12

Which executives are better trained? Which organization has more knowledgeable directors, executives, employees, customers, and suppliers?

I-13

Which executives build people? Which organization truly rewards merit and encourages personal growth?

I-14

Find the answers to these questions. They will predict which plan has the greatest chance of success.

I-15

The executive who heeds this advice is sure to succeed. Such a person should be placed in an important position. The executive who disregards this advice will fail. Such a person should be dismissed.

I-16
Taking into account the elements of competitive analysis discussed above, each executive is charged with creating plans for competitive action that leverage personal and organizational strength and minimize weakness. By competitive actions, I mean activities that bring an individual or an organization into conflict with other individuals or organizations. Leveraging strengths gives you a competitive advantage. Competitive advantage is the key to promotion and profit.

I-17
Plans are the beginning of action. But competitive advantage is gained only by effective execution. Far better to have superior execution of a mediocre plan than poor execution of a superior plan. Poor execution destroys the best of plans. Superior execution, on the other hand, makes them better. Surprise your competitors with your willingness to improve and evolve through adaptive execution as the competitive situation unfolds.

I-18
Constantly seek better approaches to effective execution of plans. Modify your methods and evolve your strategies according to competitive reality. Even after you are successful, look for new sources of strength. Nurture and grow profitable products, services, and markets.

I-19
Always maintain your good name and reputation for success in the minds of those who determine your future. Maintain

quality and value for your customers. Keep your focus on the needs of your customers.

I-20
Draw constituents to you with the exciting promise of better service and more profit. Dominate your marketplace. Deliver superior value with effective execution of well-considered plans.

I-21
Consider your competitor's position. In circumstances where your competitor is strong, find holes in his defense. Adapt your products and services to enter these market gaps. Look for signs of discontent among his constituents. Move swiftly to meet their needs.

When you competitor is weak, overwhelm him with the advantages of your products. Provide better service. Do not rest.

I-22
Confuse your competitors with constant improvements, new features, greater value. Adaptive execution is the one weapon that cannot be defeated.

I-23
Consider your competitor's attitude. When your competitor is arrogant, be humble. Find out why his constituents favor him. Be simple. Ask for advice. Careful questions will uncover his weakness.

I-24
Wear out your competition with unrelenting attention to the desires of your constituents.

I-25

Where your competitor sees only one way to fulfill a need, discover two or three more. Divide the market into smaller and more profitable segments. Think hard about how you can benefit those you serve!

I-26

Learn more about the people who use your services. Get better information. Act quickly before your competitor does it first.

I-27

These actions open the way of success. Use them. Adapt them. Profit from them.

I-28

The executive who carefully prepares before entering into competition understands how to leverage strength. With well-considered preparations, one can develop alternatives for action that offer the greatest opportunities for promotion and profit. With adaptive execution, one can turn these opportunities into ultimate victory.

Waging War

Sun Tzu said:

In order to establish an army, the general needs thousands of chariots, tens of thousands of wagons and carts, and hundreds of thousands of soldiers. Supplies must be transported over thousands of *li*. There will be expenses for officers and staff, expenses for soldiers, expenses for chariots, leather armor, arrows, spears, and swords, expenses for all manner of things. Thousands of *liang* (pieces) of gold will be expended each day to establish the army.

II

COMPETITIVE ACTIONS

II-1

Competitive actions must be supported by personal and organization resources. The most important of these resources are creativity, flexibility, and commitment.

II-2

The greater the scope of the actions, the greater the expenditure of resources. Sufficient resources should be available before action is undertaken.

II-3

The aim of competitive action should be to realize profit as quickly as possible. If profit is delayed, enthusiasm fades and resources drain away. If activities are continued for a long time without positive results, strength of will and determination to win become exhausted.

II-4
If unprofitable competitive actions are prolonged, even a large quantity of resources will not be sufficient.

II-5
When commitment is dulled by loss, when enthusiasm has faded and resources are drained away, competitors will take advantage of your weakness. Overtaken by defeat, no executive, however wise, can prevent decline of his career and loss of opportunity.

II-6
Competitive actions should proceed at a timely pace. Hastily performed operations tend to invite mistakes. But operations that waste time are never profitable. A successful competitive operation need not be complicated. To maximize profit, do simple things well, and do them at the appropriate time.

II-7
Strategies that cause mistakes or exhaust resources never produce a profit.

II-8
Executives who cannot balance risk with opportunity do not profit in a swiftly changing, uncertain market environment. Accurate information, well-considered plans, and timely execution are the keys. Only those who are comfortable with the pitfalls and ambiguities of rapid adaptation can profitably manage products and services in slippery market conditions. Only those who appreciate and use the knowledge gained from quick and inexpensive experiments and tests can achieve lasting success.

II-9

A skillful executive does not hesitate to confront the competition with resources at his command. He engages the enemy to determine strength and weakness. He gains precious information from direct contact with constituents. He does not waste time talking to anyone farther removed from the competitive arena than he is. Being one step ahead of the competition is worth more than anything else. *Gaining that step is the wise executive's greatest desire.*

II-10

A skillful executive assembles the strongest possible team from the people available to him. He observes the competition and learns how to increase the value of his own products. In this way, he is always increasing his constituent share. He builds his fortune through outstanding service.

II-11

Accurate intelligence is the foundation of profitable operations. When an executive fails, it is often due to reliance on folk wisdom. Folk wisdom is that body of unchallenged and generally incorrect assumptions perpetuated by those who lack real knowledge and information. Folk wisdom exists at every level of every organization. Rapid, profitable adaptation feeds on facts, not unsupported assumptions.

II-12

Timely, accurate intelligence is the lifeblood of successful competition. Good intelligence can be expensive to obtain. But failure is even more expensive. Develop reliable sources of high-value information.

II-13

The most costly intelligence is that which is out of date. Seventy percent of the value of intelligence is gained from timeliness. Yesterday's data are practically useless.

II-14

The wise executive harvests information at every opportunity. He learns from his constituents and his competitors. One new product idea generated from discussion with a real customer is worth any number of ideas generated by consultants or staff.

II-15

In order to dominate a market, you and your people—from top to bottom—must be passionate about the services you provide and the products you represent.

II-16

To capture the enthusiasm of your employees, you must offer them clearly defined and reasonably attainable rewards. Rewards should be meaningful on both an individual and group level. You should reward people as a group for reaching assigned common goals that are based on teamwork. But people should also be rewarded for individual merit. Different kinds of people are motivated by different types of rewards.

II-17

When someone makes an outstanding contribution to profitability, reward him openly. Make his service to the organization an example for others to follow by providing sure and valuable rewards for excellence.

II-18
Treat your employees well; train them thoroughly. The success of the organization is built on the individual success of its members. This is how you are able to dominate one situation and create the resources and expertise to seize the next opportunity.

II-19
The important thing in competitive operations is timely execution leading to quick profitability. Unnecessarily prolonged activity wastes time and resources. The executive who understands how to excite his people and dominate a marketplace will become the foundation for his company.

Military Strategy

Sun Tzu said:
In general, the best method for using military force is to conquer an entire country intact; to destroy the country is inferior. Ancient warriors who knew how to use military power defeated the enemy, but not by fighting a battle. They overpowered the enemy, but did little damage in the process. The goal of military strategy is to take things whole. In this way, soldiers are not killed and wealth is preserved. Therefore, a general who wins all his battles by destroying other armies is not the ultimate warrior. The ultimate warrior is one who wins the war without fighting any battles.

The best use of military power, then, is to use superior positioning to force a surrender. If this tactic fails, use diplomacy. After that, use military power as a threat. As a last resort, attack your enemy.

III

COMPETITIVE STRATEGY

III-1

It is better to dominate a whole organization or market with superior service and rapid execution than to splinter it with destructive tactics. To ruin a competitor is inferior to acquiring his resources intact.

III-2

Capturing a competitor's constituents is better than destroying his reputation; recruiting his productive employees is better than destroying their jobs; disrupting his distribution channels is better than tarnishing his company's image.

III-3

It does not require much skill to fight a battle. Even if you win one hundred battles in a row, you have not shown any real ability. Winning the approval of an entire constituency without fighting a battle (i.e., become a sole source or preferred provider of a product or service) is a far greater accomplishment. Those who reach this level of dominance do so with unrelenting attention to planning and execution. Instead of fighting expensive head-to-head battles, they rapidly adapt to market preferences, thereby creating superior products and services.

III-4
The ideal strategy is to make a competitor's products or services obsolete through adaptive evolution; that is, creating better products and services by a process of controlled mutation in response to observed market factors.

III-5
The next-best strategy is to improve the quality of products, services, and operations.

III-6
The *next* next-best strategy is to market yourself more effectively.

III-7
The worst strategy is to engage in destructive attacks on a competitor's reputation or products. This kind of strategy is a matter of desperation clearly lacking in sophistication and imagination. It often results in the ruin of all parties involved.

III-8
To engage in destructive competition is ultimately self-defeating. Your aim is to earn and justify the trust and confidence of your constituents. How can you do this by ruining others' reputations and demonstrating your own lack of imagination?

III-9

If an executive is unable to control his impatience and immediately seeks to destroy his competitors by direct attacks, he will waste a large part of his energy and resources without accomplishing much. The impact of such actions can be disastrous.

III-10

The skillful executive conquers with knowledge and imagination. He patiently evolves better products by uncovering unmet needs in profitable market niches. He creates greater value. He outflanks his competitors by improving market position without resorting to direct attack or drawn-out campaigns.

III-11

Your aim is to use quality and value to take over a whole segment of constituents intact. In this way, your resources will be preserved and your profit enhanced. This is the art of effective competitive strategy.

III-12

Think about competitive action in this way: If your constituent base is already five to ten times larger than your competitor's, press hard through aggressive attention to value. Dominate the market with your presence. Invest resources in adaptive evolution. Find out what the customer wants tomorrow.

III-13

If you have only twice as many constituents, make sure you understand why they are choosing your product and why they might choose your competitor's product. Talk with your own customers. Talk with your competitor's customers. Redefine and differentiate yourself. How are you different? How are you better? In what aspects are you inferior?

III-14
If your market share is equal to that of your competition, seek ways to carve the constituent group into smaller, more profitable niches that you alone can dominate. Further, seek new constituents for existing services. What other services can you provide? How is value defined in your market? Are you aligned with the definition? Where is your market going? Can you get there ahead of your competition? Look at yourself through new eyes.

III-15
If you are weaker than your competition, hold your position as long as there is some profit and a reasonable prospect for market-share improvement. Make plans to move into a more profitable position that you can dominate. Think about how many advantages flow from dominance. Greater profit is one; better morale is another. If an existing constituency is bleeding your resources, find or create another as fast as you can! A slow death is death nonetheless.

III-16
If your products or position are in all respects inferior to your competitor's, abandon them. Even strong desire and intense effort will not turn straw into gold. Invest your resources into a more promising situation.

III-17
Executive decisions can either shape success or induce failure. Executives must be leaders. If an executive is smart and

courageous, he and his organization will surely expand and prosper. If an executive is passive and weak, he and his organization will just as surely die. Success or failure is determined by executive leadership alone.

III-18
The power that flows from an executive's position should be exercised thoughtfully. An executive who does not understand how to use this power can cause major problems for himself and his organization. Here are three examples of how an executive can cause trouble by inappropriate use of executive power.

III-19
First, an executive misuses power when he decides to act out of ignorance, lacking firsthand knowledge of the competitive situation. For instance, acing out of ignorance, he could initiate competitive activities when the chances of winning are small. This leads to certain defeat. Or, acting out of ignorance, he could terminate competitive activities that are on the verge of success, thereby losing an opportunity for profit. Either way, issuing orders that are not based on a real understanding of the competitive situation causes trouble.

III-20
Second, an executive misuses power when he focuses too much attention on *process* rather than *progress*. When procedure-minded executives attempt to control activities with cumbersome rules, they choke operations and hamper profit. Aggressiveness—balanced by reason, flexibility, and imagination—fuels the kind of adaptive evolution and rapid execution that promotes success.

III-21

Third, an executive misuses power when he promotes those who lack skill or wisdom. Leaders are a critical resource. When leaders are selected using factors unrelated to ability, employees become skeptical and suspicious. This inevitably lowers morale and productivity. Effective leadership is everything! Authority must reside in the hands of those who can lead.

II-22

If employees are confused and unmotivated by misuse of executive power, competitors will steal away constituents. Executive weakness gives strength to competitors.

III-23

Five indicators predict which executive will dominate:

III-24

An executive who knows when to fight and when to retreat will win.

III-25

An executive who uses resources appropriate to the challenge at hand will win.

III-26

An executive who applies adaptive evolution and rapid execution effectively will win.

III-27

An executive who relies on accurate, timely information will win.

III-28

An executive who is not burdened by unnecessary rules or troublesome staff will win.

III-29

If you know your market, your competitors, and yourself, your strategies will not fail, even if you are challenged a hundred times.

III-30

If you know yourself only, but are ignorant of your market or your competitors, you can expect to fail as often as you succeed.

III-31

If you do not even know yourself, you will fail every time.

Strategic Considerations

Sun Tzu said:

Great warriors of ancient times first made themselves invincible. After that, they awaited the enemy's moment of vulnerability. Not being conquered depends upon oneself; conquering depends upon the actions of the enemy. Thus, a skilled warrior can remain unvanquished, but the enemy may not be vulnerable. Therefore, if one cannot conquer, he should wait. When one can conquer, only then should he attack.

Great warriors are not victorious because they possess infinite wisdom or boundless courage. Rather, great warriors are those who make no mistakes. Every strategy they employ leads to eventual victory. Thus, those who defend are invisible, as if hidden in the deepest recesses of the ninefold earth. Those who attack are invincible, as if sustained by the power of heaven. By waiting for the enemy's moment of vulnerability, they surely triumph.

IV

POSITIONING

IV-1

Effective executives position themselves and their products in situations where they will survive. Then they wait for the opportunity to attack.

IV-2

Survival depends on one's own actions; victory depends on using the opportunity provided by the actions of others.

IV-3

Therefore, while an effective executive can always survive, he may not necessarily be able to triumph.

IV-4

Thus, it is said: The path of victory may be marked, but one must walk it carefully.

Sun Tzu said:
A great general establishes a position where he cannot be defeated. He misses no opportunity to exploit the weakness of his enemy. A winning general understands how to craft victory before beginning the war. A losing general begins the war without knowing how to win it. A great commander starts by cultivating his own leadership character and developing a strong organization. In this way, he controls those factors that are crucial to his success.

Five elements comprise the art of strategy: First, measuring; second, estimating; third, calculating; fourth, comparing; and fifth, executing. The terrain creates measurements. Estimates are based on measurements. Calculations on estimates. Comparisons on estimates. And execution on comparisons. Using these five elements, a victorious army strikes its opponents like a heavy spear hurling through a bamboo curtain, or like a fierce river rushing down a narrow gorge. It cannot be stopped. Thus, success in war is a matter of timing and execution.

IV-5

Survival depends on a careful defense; victory results from seizing the initiative at the right moment.

IV-6

If your resources are not adequate to win, take a defensive approach. When the moment is right, move swiftly.

IV-7

Effective executives defend positions that cannot be attacked. Effective executives initiate actions from positions of ultimate advantage. Thus, they achieve victory without the risk of being defeated.

IV-8

To overwhelm a situation through loud confrontation or uncontrolled emotion does not indicate superior ability. After all, it takes no great skill to embarrass others into retreat if one sacrifices his own dignity.

IV-9

In the same way, it takes no great skill to win a heated argument in a public place or criticize someone when they cannot respond.

IV-10

Effective executives win victories that seem easy to those observing the action.

IV-11

Effective executives are people of normal ability. They do not possess exceptional wisdom or unrelenting courage.

IV-12
Rather, effective executives win because they make no mistakes. They are unfailingly competent. Every action they take, every tactic they employ, contributes to their eventual triumph. By waiting for others to provide the opportunity, they are always in a position to win.

IV-13
Effective executives establish positions where they can survive. Then, they miss no chance to exploit opportunities provided by their market or competition.

IV-14
A winning executive understands the conditions of victory before taking action. A losing executive takes action before knowing how to win.

IV-15
Once in a strong position, an effective executive cultivates his own leadership character and develops a responsive organization. In this way, he controls those factors that are crucial to success.

IV-16
Before seizing the initiative, he carefully considers the five elements of strategy. The elements of strategy are: first, identifying opportunity; second, gathering facts; third, analyzing alternatives; fourth, judging appropriateness; and fifth, taking action.

IV-17
The situation, i.e., the actions or decisions of others in the market or in the organization, creates opportunity.

IV-18
Facts clarify the situation. Alternatives are based on facts. Appropriateness is based on evaluation of alternatives. Action is based on picking the most appropriate alternative.

IV-19
When he takes action, an effective executive succeeds like a heavy spear hurling through a bamboo curtain or a fierce river rushing through a narrow gorge. His momentum cannot be stopped.

IV-20
The ability to triumph is a matter of timing and execution. Wait in a position where you can seize the opportunity created by others. Execute appropriate plans when the moment of action arrives.

Strategic Power

Sun Tzu said:

Fighting many foes is the same as fighting few. It is a matter of using formations and communications. Any army can fight without losing. It is a matter of mixing orthodox tactics with unorthodox tactics to keep the enemy off-balance. However, when an army overcomes the enemy like smashing eggs against a stone wall, it is a matter of emptiness and fullness, of strength against weakness. The enemy does not know where to defend and is crushed.

For a skilled commander, momentum is like a drawn crossbow. Timing is the trigger that will release the bolt with deadly effect. So, a great warrior creates momentum; then, at the right moment, he hurls his troops toward the enemy like an avalanche of rocks thundering down the side of a mountain. His victory is a matter of momentum and timing.

V

OPPORTUNITY AND TIMING

V-1

The principles used to lead a large group are the same as those used to lead a small group. It is a matter of setting up appropriate organization structure and communications.

V-2

Taking on a strong competitor is the same as taking on a weak competitor. It is a matter of creating favorable opportunities and using the power of timing.

V-3

Even an executive of average ability can manage to survive. It is a simple matter of taking reasonable actions and providing adequate service to his constituency.

V-4

But when an executive is able to dominate a situation, it is because he creates opportunity and understands timing. It is a matter of reality and illusion, hiding real strength behind the illusion of weakness. Competitors do not know what to defend against.

V-5

In competitive situations, one normally begins the battle using expected tactics so the enemy's response can be assessed. Certain victory, however, is achieved by using unexpected tactics—that is, by rapidly adapting offensive and defensive actions in response to emerging opportunities.

V-6

The executive who is skillful at using unexpected tactics has infinite resources. For him, moving from expected tactics to unexpected tactics and back again flows smoothly, like the surface of a great river.

V-7

The expected and the unexpected begin and end again, like the waxing and waning of the moon. They cycle from beginning to end, like the four seasons, each in its appointed time.

V-8

There are only five notes in the musical scale; but in a lifetime, we could not hear their infinite combinations.

V-9

There are only five colors in an artist's palette, but, in a lifetime, we could not see their infinite combinations.

V-10

There are only five flavors in cooking; but, in a lifetime, we could not taste their infinite combinations.

V-11

The evolution of competitive activities gives rise to opportunities to use both expected and unexpected tactics. We could not in a lifetime exploit all the possibilities provided by crafting tactics based on weaving the expected with the unexpected.

V-12

Expected and unexpected tactics evolve from each other during the ebb and flow of conflict, like a circle with no starting point. Your opponent cannot tell where one begins and the other ends.

V-13

When rushing water carries huge boulders, it is because of overwhelming power.

V-14

But, when the diving falcon breaks the neck of its prey, it is because of precise timing.

V-15

For the skilled executive, opportunity reveals the target and timing is the trigger that unleashes the power to conquer.

V-16

The skilled executive creates opportunity by putting intense pressure on his competitor. When his competitor stumbles, he times his attack to produce unfailing victory.

V-17
Amidst the chaos of organizational politics or the competitive marketplace, the skilled executive is able to detect patterns in the activities of his rivals. He, on the other hand, carefully disguises his own objectives. He moves resources around in seemingly random ways, almost as if he is wandering in circles. He appears confused and arbitrary, but he cannot be defeated.

V-18
This kind of apparent disorder can only be the outcome of expert organization and precise communication. The illusion of fear and confusion can only come from great courage. Seeming weakness is a function of realized strength.

V-19
The skilled executive maneuvers his opponents. He creates favorable opportunities by luring his competitors into vulnerable positions with the promise of easy gains. Then, he waits, patiently and silently, with overwhelming power derived from combining the expected with the unexpected, the obvious and the disguised, for the moment of victory.

V-20
This is the way the skilled executive crafts his success. He does not depend upon others for advancement.

V-21
Further, the skilled executive employs the only most appropriate people to carry out his purposes at the critical moment.

V-22
People must be employed according to their ability and temperament. Some are more suited than others for the stress

and ambiguity of competition. Use people who can achieve your objectives under difficult conditions.

V-23
Thus, a skilled executive creates circumstances that operate in his favor; then, at the right moment, he strikes his opponent like an avalanche of rocks thundering down the side of a mountain.

Emptiness and Fullness

Sun Tzu said:

A skilled warrior moves his opponent; he does not allow his opponent to move him. Against a skilled attacker, the enemy does not know where to defend. Against a skilled defender, the enemy does not know where to attack. When we seem formless and invisible, we become the arbiter of the enemy's fate. One is strong if he forces the enemy to respond; one is weak if he must respond to the enemy.

Therefore, a great general ensnares the enemy while retaining his own freedom. He creates an overwhelming advantage where the enemy is weak. According to my way of thinking, even if an opponent outnumbers me, how will this help him win if I control the situation?

VI

CONTROL

VI-1

Those who prepare quickly and thoroughly await the encounter at ease; those who try to catch up are rushed and exhausted.

VI-2

A skilled executive moves his competition; he does not allow them to move him.

VI-3

A skilled executive lures his competitor into advancing by creating the illusion of false advantage; he discourages his competitor from attacking by erecting fake barriers. Hence, his competitor advances toward failure and retreats from success.

VI-4
A skilled executive keeps his rivals on the move and in the dark. If a competitor becomes comfortable, he creates difficulty. If a competitor is satisfied, he creates a problem. If a competitor is calm, he creates chaos.

VI-5
A skilled executive appears suddenly where the competition must rush to defend against him. He occupies places where the competition least expects to find him.

VI-6
A skilled executive positions his resources with ease because he begins his campaign by occupying territory not contested by others.

VI-7
A skilled executive's offensive actions always succeed because he attacks points which cannot be defended. A skilled executive's defensive positions never fail because he defends points which cannot be attacked.

VI-8
Against such an offensive, the competition cannot know where to defend. Against such a defense, the competition cannot know where to attack.

VI-9
The best strategies are subtle. They have no discernable form. The best strategies are obscured. They cannot be penetrated. When formless and impenetrable, one controls a competitor's destiny.

VI-10
When a skilled executive pressures his opponent, he concentrates on weak points and cannot be stopped. When a skilled executive changes position, he moves swiftly and cannot be deterred.

VI-11
If it is time for an encounter, pull your competitor into the fray. Even if he hides behind a wall of money or power, he must respond if a valuable product or critical market is threatened.

VI-12
If it is not time for an encounter, even if a competitor is strong and able, he can do no harm if he has nothing to aim at.

VI-13
A skilled executive compels the competition to respond while retaining his own initiative. He divides the competition while he remains intact. He distracts the competition while he remains focused. He applies major pressure to points that are defended with few resources. He creates overwhelming leverage. He concentrates strength against weakness.

VI-14
The less a competitor knows about where we intend to concentrate our attention, the stronger we become. If a competitor must spread his resources across a wide front, each place he defends will be weaker. Eventually, he will be unable to meet our challenge.

Sun Tzu said:

Victory can be crafted. Even if the enemy is mighty, I can make him lose his will to fight. Therefore, I probe carefully to determine which strategies can succeed and which will fail. I spar with the enemy to determine when he will defend and when he will attack. I assume various positions to determine where he is strong and where he is weak. I compare my forces with his to determine relative sufficiency and insufficiency.

When I develop my strategy, I make it formless and invisible. A formless strategy cannot be grasped; an invisible strategy cannot be seen. I defeat the enemy by controlling the situation, but he has no idea how I control it. Even though all can see afterwards how the battle was won, none should understand the reasoning I applied to create the method of victory.

VI-15

If we force a competitor to strengthen one department, he must weaken another. If he strengthens one product, he weakens another. If he concentrates on one constituency, he must ignore another. If he tries to be strong everywhere, he will certainly be weak somewhere.

VI-16

One is strong if he causes the competition to react to him; one is weak if he must react to the competition.

VI-17

If an executive controls the time and place of an encounter, he can make careful preparations and minimize the risk of failure. If one does not control the time and place of battle, no matter how many resources are thrown into the conflict, preparations will be inadequate and failure will occur.

VI-18

According to my way of thinking, if I control the situation, how can a competitor use his resources effectively, even if they are greatly superior?

VI-19

So it is said: With control, victory can be crafted by those with skill. Even if the enemy is strong, with control, I can make him lose his will to fight.

VI-20

Therefore, I carefully probe to determine which strategies can win and which will lose.

VI-21

I spar with the competition to determine what points they will defend and where they will attack.

VI-22

I assume various positions to determine where they are strong and where they are weak.

VI-23

I compare my resources with their resources to determine relative strength and weakness.

VI-24

When I develop my final strategy, I make sure it is formless and invisible. A formless strategy cannot be discovered; an invisible strategy cannot be defeated.

VI-25

I overwhelm the competition by controlling the situation, but my opponents cannot figure out how I do it. Even though all can see that victory was achieved, none can understand the way it was done. My results become apparent while my methods remain hidden.

VI-26

Successful strategies should not be repeated. Each conflict represents a unique situation. And predictability foreshadows defeat.

VI-27

Successful strategies flow like water; they adapt themselves to the circumstances of the conflict. When water flows, it avoids the high ground and seeks the low. Successful strategies likewise avoid the enemy's strength and find his weakness.

VI-28
Just as the flow of water adapts to the contour of the land, the flow of victory adapts to the actions of the opponent.

VI-29
Just as water assumes the shape of any container holding it, the tactics of victory must assume the shape of the present situation.

VI-30
By observing nature, we see continuous variation and cycles of change. Nothing remains the same in every situation. Nor is one aspect of nature superior to another in every circumstance. Each of the four seasons appears in turn and each has its advantages. Some days are longer and some days are shorter. The moon waxes and wanes.

VI-31
In the same way, the skilled executive crafts his victory by adapting his plans and resources to the place and time of the encounter. He matches his strength against his opponent's weakness. His victory is called a stroke of genius.

Maneuvering the Army

Sun Tzu said:

Nothing is more difficult than maneuvering the army. Maneuvering successfully depends on misdirecting the enemy and luring them away from your objective. Doing this, even if you start later than the enemy, you will arrive on the battlefield first. Direct your forces to take up advantageous positions. Retain freedom of action. He who is able to move without restriction will win.

Skilled warriors win by using deception. The secret of deception is to manipulate the enemy's perceptions. Make the far away seem near and the near seem far away. Make the direct seem indirect and the indirect seem direct.

VII

MANAGING ENGAGEMENT

VII-1
Once an executive decides to engage the competition, he must gather his resources, organize them carefully, and bring them under his control.

VII-2
The most difficult aspect of competition on any level is managing a direct engagement with a competitor. Winning in a direct engagement depends on controlling information effectively. In planning an engagement, gather information from your competitor and from the marketplace. Determine where the real advantages and disadvantages lie. Uncover what is real and what is illusion.

VII-3
Further, muddle up the information you broadcast to your competitor. Muddled information will misdirect your com-

petitor and lead him astray. You can encourage him to adopt a less-effective strategy by creating false perceptions. Thus, even if you start out later than your competitor, you will arrive first. Only those who understand the subtleties of controlling information can achieve this.

VII-4
Direct engagement can be used to gain an advantage; or, direct engagement can be used to avoid a loss.

VII-5
If your goal is to gain an advantage, then timing is critical. Do not create an unwieldy organization that utilizes unnecessary resources. This will slow you down. Remember, rapid execution of an effective plan is the key. If you move slowly, your competitor will escape and whatever opportunity you had will be lost.

VII-6
On the other hand, do not fragment your organization or fail to provide important resources to advance in the name of speed.

VII-7
If you skip over necessary preparation and move hastily into a difficult engagement, even if you work day and night, you will have little chance of success. Your efforts will be scattered. Your resources will be wasted. Your motivation will be destroyed.

VII-8
Adequate preparation—determining what mix of resources to apply at what time—is essential to success in a direct engagement. It is unwise to risk engagement unprepared.

VII-9

If you lack relevant training or proper equipment, your engagement will be defeated. If you lack critical financial support, your engagement will be defeated. If you lack timely, accurate information, your engagement will be defeated.

VII-10

The executive who does not know his competitor's objectives, resources, and allies cannot know with whom to form alliances. If he does not know the minds of his constituents and the political and market environments, he cannot focus his resources.

VII-11

If an executive does not employ every means to discover his opponent's strengths and weaknesses—including informants, spies, and turncoats—he cannot hope to develop workable strategies.

VII-12

Succeeding in a direct engagement on a competitor depends on deceiving him. If your stratagems are obvious to your competitor, no matter how good they are, he can defeat them. Concentrate on your objective, but develop your strategy in secret. Keep your competitor off-balance by constantly changing form.

VII-13

In this way, your methods are hidden. You are free to move as fiercely as a winter storm or as gently as a summer breeze. You can attack like a roaring fire. You can stand firm like an unshakeable mountain. You can strike like lightning, a sear-

Sun Tzu said:
A skilled general does not attack when the enemy's spirits are high. He attacks when the enemy is tired. A skilled general waits for the enemy to come to him from afar. Do not attack a well-ordered formation. Do not advance up a hill. Do not retreat down a slope. Do not pursue a false retreat. Do not attack crack troops. Do not take the enemy's bait. Do not intercept an enemy who is returning home. When you surround an enemy, give him a way out. Do not press a desperate enemy. This is the essence of managing engagement.

ing bolt of force from the darkness piercing to the heart of your opponent's weakness.

VII-14
Confuse your opponent's focus and you will be able to harvest his constituency. Cause him to lose his direction and you will conquer.

VII-15
If you can move without restriction while hampering the movements of your competitor, you will win.

VII-16
The secret of winning a direct engagement is knowing how to manipulate perceptions. Make distant threats seem near and nearby threats seem distant. Make unprofitable strategies seem reasonable and profitable strategies seem unworkable.

VII-17
Direct engagements and other critical situations generate intense emotions. In circumstances where emotions run high, rational thinking may suffer. Further, clear communication among members of your group may be blocked.

VII-18
For these reasons, during intense situations, use devices that will minimize distraction and reduce chaos by refocusing attention on objectives. If your employees are unified by clear communication during critical moments, those who are bold will not attempt unwise initiatives and those who are timid will not ignore opportunity or shrink from the fray. This is the way people are managed during crises.

VII-19
Remember, however, that your messages and signals to each other might be intercepted by your competitors. Therefore, confuse your opponents by mixing false signals with real ones. But fooling your opponents requires a high level of discipline and commitment among members of your group.

VII-20
Watching a competitor's actions can provide the means to demotivate his manpower and distract him from his purpose.

VII-21
If you observe a competitor closely, you will see that his spirit is often high in the early stages of engagement. Later, his spirit will diminish. As matters drag on further, he will become anxious for a resolution. Use this trend to your advantage.

VII-22
Avoid a competitor when his spirits are high. Pressure him when he is lazy or tired. Time your actions according to his level of energy.

VII-23
Face a chaotic competitor with discipline. Meet a disordered competitor with calm. In this way, you control your own emotions.

VII-24
Wait for a competitor to come to you. Gather critical information. Analyze it in-depth. In this way, you will be thoroughly prepared.

VII-25

Do not be in a hurry to engage a well-prepared competitor. Do not challenge a well-managed group in haste. Wait for the situation to change.

VII-26

Manage engagements in this way. Do not challenge strong, easily defended products or positions. This will force you to retreat.

VII-27

Do not pursue a competitor when he appears to move away from a strong position. This may be a false retreat designed to entrap you.

VII-28

Do not attack a competitor's sharpest people unless you have an overwhelming advantage.

VII-29

Do not snatch at an apparent advantage without investigation. You may fall into a hidden pit.

VII-30

If a competitor is voluntarily withdrawing from your market, do not chase him. He is already defeated.

VII-31

When a competitor has exhausted his resources in battle, give him a way out. Let him retain his ability to earn a living. Do not attempt to destroy him completely. This may prove to be a costly act.

VII-32
There is no need to press a desperate competitor. Desperation itself will cause defeat.

VII-33
This is the essence of managing engagement in order to win.

The Nine Possibilities

Sun Tzu said:

Only a general who is flexible and knows how to adapt his strategy to changing circumstances can command victorious troops. Therefore, do not garrison troops in abandoned lands. Unite with allies where roads intersect. Do not linger in desperate ground. Make contingency plans in surrounded land. Fight if attacked in dead lands. Do not assume the enemy will not come. Prepare for his coming. Do not assume the enemy will not attack. Rely instead on a strong defense.

VIII

ADAPTATION

VIII-1
Once an executive has decided to engage in competitive actions, he should follow these rules.

VIII-2
Do not set up a position that is politically or economically isolated, or that is far from necessary resources.

VIII-3
Do not set up a position that has many weak points and is difficult to defend or reinforce.

VIII-4
Maintain open communication with allies and provide a means for mutual support.

VIII-5
Make contingency plans in case the competition moves quickly or unexpectedly in response to your activities.

VIII-6
If pressed for immediate action, be prepared to delay engagement until you are ready.

VIII-7
When making strategic choices, for political or economic reasons, there will always be certain desirable targets that should not be attacked; some effective methods that should not be used; some incendiary issues that should not be argued; and some rich markets that should not be entered. Avoid these choices for practical reasons.

VIII-8
Further, in the midst of competitive actions, it is sometimes necessary to disregard the suggestions of highly placed individuals. Ill-considered advice should be ignored.

VIII-9
Only an executive who is flexible enough to adapt his strategy to changes in competitive circumstances can effectively manage resources during competitive operations.

VIII-10
An executive who is not flexible enough to adapt his strategy to changes in circumstances, even if he has wide knowledge of people and methods, will not be able to take advantage of this knowledge.

VIII-11

An executive who is not flexible enough to adapt his strategy to changes in circumstances, even if he recognizes an advantageous opportunity, will not be able to assign the right person to take the right action at the right time.

VIII-12

A skilled executive considers how to increase the opportunity for gain and how to decrease the possibility of loss in his strategic calculations.

VIII-13

By increasing the opportunity for gain, his plans can be trusted to yield the maximum profit; by decreasing the possibility of loss, he can foresee problems and modify his plans to overcome them.

VIII-14

A skilled executive creates hurdles for competitors in order to make their situation more difficult and discourage them from movement.

VIII-15

He creates minor irritations to keep his competitor annoyed and upset. He presents meaningless opportunities that keep his competitor occupied and his focus distracted.

VIII-16

So, to be successful in competition, do not assume your competitor will be passive. Instead, rely on careful preparation, effective planning, and a strong defense to assure your victory.

Sun Tzu said:

There are five character flaws that are dangerous for a general: If he is reckless, his men can be killed. If he is cowardly, his army can be captured. If he is short-tempered, he will react in anger. If he is self-important, he can be deceived. If he is attached to his men, he will hesitate at a critical moment. These five flaws are certainly unfortunate for a general because they cause great destruction in war. These five flaws cause generals to fail and armies to die. Consider them well.

VIII-17

Utilize the character flaws of your opponents in order to defeat them. Look for these five traits.

VIII-18

If an opponent is reckless, we can cause him to waste his resources.

VIII-19

If an opponent is timid, we can seize his resources.

VIII-20

If an opponent is short-tempered, we can cause him to be rash.

VIII-21

If an opponent is self-important, we can deceive him with flattery.

VIII-22

If an opponent is overly concerned about loss of position or reputation, he will hesitate before making a difficult decision at a critical moment.

VIII-23

These character flaws greatly restrict an executive's potential success. They are the cause of loss in competitive engagements.

VIII-24

These character flaws cause executives to fail and companies to die. Eliminate them in yourself.

Deploying Troops

Sun Tzu said:

Use the following rules. Cross mountains by following valleys. Stay on the high ground where you have a clear view of the surrounding country. Do not face uphill to fight. When the enemy is crossing water, it is advantageous to attack when half of his troops have crossed over. When crossing a swamp, move quickly. Keep away from gorges, hollows, and crevices that form natural traps and snares. If the enemy's troops must lean on their weapons in order to stand upright, they are hungry. If the enemy's water carriers drink first, the entire troop is thirsty. If enemy troops clamor during the night, the enemy is nervous and fearful. When the enemy feeds his war horses grain and kills his pack horses for meat, when the enemy's soldiers do not hang up their cooking pots nor return to their shelters, the enemy is desperate.

IX

MANEUVERING

IX-1

When the time comes to begin an engagement, use the following rules. Move around obstacles and difficulties, rather than confronting them. Gather together knowledgeable people, organize them appropriately, train them thoroughly, and equip them well.

IX-2

Do not enter into difficult circumstances with inadequate resources.

IX-3

If you must reorganize your group before an engagement, do so quickly. Move toward stability. When the competition is reorganizing, do not challenge him when he begins because he will simply revert to his former structure in order to meet you. It is more advantageous to wait until reorganization is halfway complete and all is in chaos. He cannot move forward nor can he move back.

IX-4
If you are in the midst of intense competition, do not institute large-scale organizational change yourself. Stick with acceptable, easily understood methods and procedures. Maintain traditional organization patterns and relationships.

IX-5
Keep administrative matters simple, clear, and flexible. Do not waste people's time with cumbersome procedures.

IX-6
You can manage engagements more easily when your emotions, your staff, and your operating structure are under control.

IX-7
Different competitive challenges will require that you change and adapt your tactics in order to succeed. But as far as possible, maintain balance during engagements and conflict situations. Do things the easy, well-understood way. Operate from positions that can be defended.

IX-8
Most people like balance. People work better with familiar methods, procedures, and equipment. They are more comfortable if they feel they know what is going on. They dislike feeling uninformed. Uninformed people always create dark and fearful images of the future. When people are comfortable, however, they can maintain enthusiasm and motivation. Enthusiasm and motivation are necessary for competitive success.

IX-9
When you face a challenge or obstacle, focus on the benefits of overcoming it. Generate enthusiasm with optimism. Rapidly changing or highly uncertain engagements are particularly difficult to manage. If you can, delay activities and commitments until the flood of change or uncertainty has subsided.

IX-10
In this way, your group will draw strength from your example.

IX-11
Rapidly changing or highly uncertain situations give rise to opinions. Opinions without facts are based on "folk wisdom." Folk wisdom is composed of commonly accepted but unproven assertions, myths, guesses, and speculation. Challenge the validity of folk wisdom, particularly in situations of competitive stress.

IX-12
Stay away from folk wisdom as a basis for taking action. If your competitor bases his movements on it, encourage him to continue as far as possible. Most folk wisdom is unreliable and ill-considered, so an opponent who bases his strategy on it is greatly weakened.

IX-13
When you must operate in an environment where the movements or tactics of the competition are obscured or difficult to understand, be particularly careful to watch for traps or ambushes. Challenge anything that appears unusual or out of character.

Sun Tzu said:

In war, we do not need the largest army to win. It is important not to advance recklessly. If we concentrate our forces so they match those of the enemy, if we respect the enemy's strength and carefully study his movements, we will win. If we underestimate the enemy and do not consider the meaning of his movements, we will lose.

IX-14

Before entering an engagement, study your competitor closely. Consider these things: If your competitor is ready to attack, but remains still, it is likely he has some critical advantage to rely on—look for it. If your competitor seems unprepared for conflict, but he still challenges you, he wants you to advance, leaving behind your defensive positions. There is a hidden agenda here. Investigate it thoroughly.

IX-15

If there is unexplained activity in the market or agitation among members of your constituency, your competitor may be moving behind a screen or using surrogates.

IX-16

When your competitor springs traps and creates obstacles, he is trying to confuse you. If ordinarily supportive constituents suddenly distance themselves from you, your competitor has organized a secret attack.

IX-17

Watch for signs from your competitor's group. If there is a great deal of erratic activity, he may be preparing to move quickly. If the activity level is steady and organized, he is making careful preparations. Look for patterns of activity that predict where he is focusing attention.

IX-18

If your competitor's communications sound self-effacing, but he is still confident, he is preparing to advance.

IX-19
If your competitor's communications are evasive but aggressive in tone, he is preparing to withdraw.

IX-20
If your competitor prepares a generous offer for you to consider, he may be playing for time.

IX-21
Similarly, if your competitor suddenly, and without any apparent reason, offers peace negotiations, he is plotting.

IX-22
If your competitor deploys his resources aggressively, he is expecting an engagement fairly soon.

IX-23
If your competitor feints an advance and then retreats, he is trying to lure you into making a response.

IX-24
If your competitor uses trickery or subterfuge to sustain his power, he is dealing with a critical threat.

IX-25
If you allow your competitor an obvious opening, but he fails to advance, he is tired or weak.

IX-26
If your competitor wanders aimlessly, he is uncertain.

IX-27
If your competitor speaks loudly, he is afraid.

IX-28

If your competitor's group is in turmoil, his leadership is not effective.

IX-29

If your competitor's communications channels are in disarray, his response to a crisis will be chaotic.

IX-30

If your competitor's representatives are short-tempered, they are under emotional stress.

IX-31

When your competitor uses his last available reserves to challenge you, he is desperate.

IX-32

When your competitor's people whisper among themselves in clandestine groups, your competitor is losing their loyalty.

IX-33

When your competitor hands out too many rewards, he has lost the ability to motivate his people. When your competitor hands out too many punishments, he has lost control of his people.

IX-34

When your competitor publicly criticizes his staff, he is not very smart.

IX-35

When a competitor confronts you as if prepared to attack, but neither advances forward nor retreats backward, you must study the situation carefully. Search for the important factors you have overlooked.

IX-36
In an engagement, we do not necessarily need to have the most resources to win. It is important, however, that we use resources wisely and do not challenge others recklessly.

IX-37
If you understand your competitor's strength, concentrate your resources on his weakness, and carefully study his movements, you will win. If you underestimate a competitor's strength and do not consider the meaning of his movements, you will lose.

IX-38
When managing people, if you criticize an individual before he feels loyalty to you, he will not obey your orders in the future. Further, once you have established a bond with an individual, if discipline is not enforced, he will not follow orders, either. Without obedience, it is hard to employ people effectively.

IX-39
Therefore, if you direct your employees through an appropriate organizational structure and maintain control through appropriate discipline, your people will be competent.

IX-40
If your train and motivate your employees with clear expectations, they can be relied on in critical situations. If you

train and motivate your group with vague expectations, they will fail you.

IX-41
When expectations are clear and organizational structure is appropriate for the task, people trust their leaders and submit to control.

Terrain Assessment

Sun Tzu said:

We describe terrain as accessible, ensnaring, suspending, narrow, mountainous, and remote. If the forces of both sides can enter and leave the battlefield without difficulty, then the terrain is *accessible*. If it is easy for our forces to enter the battlefield, but difficult to withdraw, then the terrain is *entrapping*. If forces from both sides have difficulty entering and leaving the battlefield, then the terrain is *suspending*. *Narrow* battlefields have restricted access routes, such as through constricted passes or deep valleys. On a *mountainous* battlefield, if our forces arrive first, take position on high ground. *Remote* battlefields are equally risky for both sides.

X

ASSESSING COMPETITIVE SITUATIONS AND CAUSES OF FAILURE

X-1

We can describe six competitive situations as accessible, ensnaring, inconclusive, restricted, difficult, and speculative.

X-2

If all competitors can reach a given constituency or market easily, then the situation is *accessible*. When the situation is accessible, try to establish a strong position first; this will give you an advantage.

X-3

If it is easy for either side to enter into a competitive engagement but difficult to withdraw, once involved, then the situation is *ensnaring*. Under these conditions, when your competitor is unprepared, you can challenge him. Remember, however, that once you are involved, your investment may become excessive, and you may not be able to withdraw without significant additional cost. Therefore, if your competitor is already positioned, it may be advantageous to avoid him. If you cannot get there first, look for an easier target.

X-4

If both sides have difficulty entering and leaving a competitive situation, then neither side may be able to win. The situation is *inconclusive*. Do not challenge a competitor when you are not confident of winning, even if he is weak. It is a waste of resources. Instead, make your competitor waste *his* resources by allow him easy access to unprofitable markets or unresponsive constituencies. Wait for another opportunity.

X-5

Restricted markets are difficult to access. Stringent technological requirements, professional knowledge, financial demands, or the like present significant barriers to entry. If you are able to enter a restricted market first, build even stronger barriers—technological, economic, and legislative—if possible. In this position, you have the advantage and can afford to await your competitor's challenge. If your competitor has already strongly established his position in this area, he has a significant advantage. Do not engage him unless he has left an opening.

X-6

Where both sides are facing a *difficult* situation and cannot readily access a market or constituency, if you are able to make inroads first, set up a strong defensive position and wait for your competitor to advance. If your competitor has already established a position, try to make it unprofitable by getting him to waste money defending it. But, do not move in too quickly if he begins to retreat. This may be a ploy.

X-7

Speculative competitive situations involve important or profitable constituents who are unknown or remote. These situations are problematic for all parties because they require taking risks whose costs and consequences are largely unclear. In a speculative situation, it is usually difficult to understand what is needed to ensure victory. Therefore, it is generally not advantageous to advance.

X-8

These are the principles for assessing the six different types of competitive situations. When an executive begins to move resources toward an objective, he must carefully examine his campaign in light of these principles.

X-9

During competitive engagements, failure can spring from six different conditions. These conditions are created not by fate, but by executive mistakes. The six conditions are: lack of resources, lack of direction, lack of performance, lack of discipline, lack of order, and lack of competence.

X-10

If all other things are equal, and an executive orders a poorly equipped, poorly supplied, poorly trained, poorly organized, or poorly funded group to challenge another group that is adequate in these areas, the cause of failure is *lack of resources*. No amount of courage or determination can make up for lack of critical resources.

X-11
If the people in a group are strong-willed but their managers are weak, the cause of failure is *lack of direction*. The group will do what it wants rather than what is intended.

X-12
If a group's managers are strong-willed but the people are poorly trained or unmotivated, the cause of failure is *lack of performance*. This is like pushing wet spaghetti uphill.

X-13
When operating executives are angry or defiant, or when they become emotional and challenge competitors without receiving orders, the cause of failure is *lack of discipline*. People act without authority.

X-14
When the chief executive is weak and lacks personal authority, when he cannot motivate people and morale is poor, or when people's responsibilities are unclear and organizational structure is vague, the cause of failure is *lack of order*. Internal confusion distracts from external objectives.

X-15
When the chief executive cannot develop effective operating plans, when he misunderstands competitors' actions, or when he underestimates the resources needed to complete engagements, the cause of failure is *lack of competence*. The overall effectiveness of a group reflects the competence of the chief executive.

X-16
These six conditions lead to failure. Every executive needs to investigate them carefully and remove them from himself.

X-17
Understanding the competitive situation can be of great advantage to a skilled executive. A skilled executive understands his constituents, his opponent, himself, and the realities all parties face, and thereby he controls victory. He correctly estimates the difficulty of alternate strategies and calculates the resources required. He accurately assesses those factors that require his attention immediately and those that can be dealt with later. He knows the strengths, weaknesses, and capacity of the people involved in the situation—both his own and those loyal to his opponent. A skilled executive wins because he takes the time to know all these things and applies his knowledge to take advantage of opportunities presented.

X-18
Therefore, if a skilled executive calculates that success is probable, he should go ahead, even if his advisors think differently. If he calculates failure, he should stop, even if his advisors want him to move.

X-19
An executive who competes, but does not seek personal glory; who acts, but does not seek to avoid responsibility; whose only goal is to benefit his constituents and his organization, is a company's most precious asset.

X-20
Treat your associates like your own family and they will strive for you. Treat them like your beloved friends and they will repay you with loyalty.

X-21
But if you become so generous with your associates and employees that you cannot manage them, so kind you cannot maintain order or direct them when they are confused, it is like spoiling your children. Once spoiled, they are not effective.

X-22
In deciding what time to begin my actions, I use the following guidelines. If I know my group has the resources to succeed but I do not know whether my competitor is vulnerable, then my chances of victory are half at this point.

X-23
If I know my competitor is vulnerable but I do not know if my group has the resources to succeed, my chances of victory are half.

X-24
If I know my competitor is vulnerable and I know my group has the resources to succeed but I do not know if the competitive situation allows me to win, my chances of victory are also half.

X-25

Hence, those executives who experience success advance only when they know the time is right; as a result, they have no need to retreat.

X-26

Know your opponent and know yourself; you will not lose. Know the competitive situation and the constituents involved also; then your success will be complete.

The Ninefold Earth

Sun Tzu said:

The battlefield situation determines whether it is more advantageous to advance or to withdraw. In a scattered situation, avoid a fight. In an uncommitted situation, keep the elements of the army in close contact with each other. In a competitive situation, do not attack. In an accessible situation, do not cease to be diligent. In an intersecting situation, consolidate your alliances. In a critical situation, seize important positions. In a surrounded situation, block access routes. In a deadly situation, tell the army it may not survive.

XI

ADAPTATION AND OFFENSIVE STRATEGY

XI-1

Proper application of the principles of offensive strategy requires analysis of the competitive situation. The competitive situation determines what type of adaptation is necessary in order to win. The competitive situation determines whether we should attack or defend, how we can best employ our resources, and what route to take. There are nine different competitive situations. These situations must be examined carefully.

XI-2

When a competitor challenges our position before we can concentrate our resources to defend it, we are in a *scattered situation*.

XI-3

If we are beginning to advance into a competitor's territory, but have expended few resources in the process, we are in an *uncommitted situation*.

XI-4

In a *scattered situation*, avoid a fight. Concentrate your resources to multiply their power. Keep the competition at bay until you are prepared. In an *uncommitted situation*, match the outflow of resources with the expected benefits of success to maintain competitive flexibility.

XI-5

If we have established a profitable position in a market that is also profitably occupied by our competitor, we are in a *conflict situation*.

XI-6

If we can advance and retreat easily, but it is also easy for our for our competition to advance and retreat, we are in an *accessible situation*.

XI-7

In a *conflict situation*, do not advance into a competitor's strength. Instead, approach from the blind side; create some kind of advantage before expending resources. In an *accessible situation*, keep your guard up. You can be attacked from any direction. Plan your defenses carefully.

XI-8

If the position we occupy overlaps several constituencies, and allows us to tap into the different markets represented by these constituencies, we are in an *intersecting situation*.

XI-9

When we have penetrated deeply into another's territory and have expended large amounts of resources to do so, we are in a *critical situation*.

XI-10

In an *intersecting situation*, consolidate your resources. Focus on overlapping market areas to achieve penetration into multiple constituencies. In a *critical situation*, take important positions first. Make sure your technical, financial, and organizational resources are adequate to hold them.

XI-11

When we must overcome technical, financial, or organizational difficulties before proceeding, or there are major barriers to reaching the constituents we want, we are in a *blocked situation*.

XI-12

When we continue to commit resources to influence constituents and cannot withdraw without sustaining a loss, but several competitors have already been successful in eroding our market position, we are in a *surrounded situation*.

XI-13

When we can survive only if we challenge competitors and win a quick victory, but will perish if we delay or if we are defeated, we are in a *deadly situation*.

XI-14

In a *blocked situation*, break out quickly. Focus on weak points in obstacles and punch through them. In a *surrounded situation*, hinder your competitor's ability to maneuver by limiting access to your position and constituents. At the same time, ex-

Sun Tzu said:

The business of the commanding general is to bring all the forces together and put them into a dangerous situation. Lead troops by your actions, not by your words. The troops of those skilled in leadership behave like the "Simultaneously Responding" serpent. The "Simultaneously Responding" serpent lives in the mountains of Chang. If its head is threatened, its tail will swiftly attack. If its tail is threatened, its head will attack. If its body is threatened, both the head and tail will attack at the same time. In the same fashion, the goal of leadership is to make the soldiers think and fight as one team.

ecute a strategy to break out of the trap. In a *deadly situation*, face the fact that you may not survive. Advance quickly; expend your resources trying to win through and escape. The alternative is a slow but sure death.

XI-15
In managing competitive engagements, skilled executives make it difficult for competitors to defend all aspects of their positions. They make it difficult for competitors to coordinate the use of resources. They make it difficult for competitors to support weaker organizational elements, leaving them vulnerable to attack. They make it difficult for competitors to communicate with constituents.

XI-16
When a competitor's resources are spread thinly, skilled executives prevent their concentration. When a competitor's resources are concentrated, skilled executives focus on undefended areas.

XI-17
Skilled executives use resources to advance when it is profitable to advance and they stop when it is not.

XI-18
You may well ask at this point: "How can I defeat a well-prepared, well-managed competitor who is about to confront me?" The answer is: Get something the competitor wants. Then he will comply with your desires.

XI-19
Quick, effective adaptation is the major factor in successful competitive actions. You must take advantage of opportu-

nities in the situation before your competitor arrives. Exploit his lack of readiness. Punish his lack of flexibility.

XI-20

In general, serious competitive engagements will succeed only if people are wholly committed to plans and goals. When people are committed, they act with unified purpose. When they have unified purpose, no defender can stop them, no attacker can overcome them. The nature of people is to ardently strive to reach any goal to which they are committed. Put your organization into a situation where they have no choice but to commit to your goals, and they will succeed beyond their imagined limits.

XI-21

When you move into a market, study your competitor's methods. Use the history of his strategies, successes, and failures to avoid making your own mistakes.

XI-22

Keep your people healthy. Save their energy for important tasks. Cherish their morale. Do not overburden them unnecessarily. Carefully plan how to use your personnel. In this way, you will be prepared to adapt to changing circumstances and reap the benefits of unexpected opportunities.

XI-23

Lead your organization to where you want to go by setting the example. Give your people no alternative—either they attain the goals you have set or they fail completely. For if the only alternative is failure, what worthwhile person will not do his best to succeed? When worthwhile people are committed to plans and goals, they do not fear failure. When they are focused in common purpose, they are calm. When they are deeply involved in their work, they have no thought but to succeed.

XI-24

Under the discipline of commitment, worthwhile people stay alert to signs of change. They follow plans and direction without compulsion. They work diligently without promises or guarantees.

XI-25

On the day a major competitive initiative is announced, even worthwhile people may voice doubts about its outcome because they realize how much effort will be needed for eventual success.

XI-26

But, if they find themselves with backs up against the wall and with reputation and advancement dependent on performance, they will exceed expectations because they must be committed.

XI-27

You may ask: "How can people in my organization become committed and cooperative?" The answer is: Force them to adopt a common cause. It is normal for people within an organization to disagree, to attempt to outdo each other. But, throw them together into a lifeboat battered by a storm and they will help each other survive in the same way that the right hand helps the left, because they are attached to the same body.

XI-28

Once you begin serious competitive activities, you cannot depend on a large organization or abundant funding for success. Only people can make it happen.

XI-29

The object of leadership is to make people work together to achieve desirable outcomes. A thorough understanding of the competitive situation will reveal how to structure both weaker and stronger, more willing and less willing elements of your organization so that all will cooperate with the plan.

XI-30

Cooperation among organizational elements is essential to success. The skilled executive creates discipline and cohesion through commitment. Therefore, he can command the whole organization as if he were commanding one person. He does this by communicating the essential aspects of his plans to the appropriate people and managing execution with clear and direct orders.

XI-31

He does not, however, allow everyone in his organization to know the complete details of his plans. In this way, his competitor is not forewarned.

XI-32

He also squelches speculation and kills harmful rumors among his employees and constituents. In this way, he controls focus and minimizes negative influences on morale.

XI-33

During execution, he changes direction and alters methods. In this way, it is difficult to anticipate direction and destination of actions; it is difficult for the competition to adapt their strategy.

XI-34

He modifies his positions and uses indirect approaches. In this way, the competition does not understand the full scope of his plans until it is too late to counter them.

XI-35

The business of the executive in command of a competitive engagement is to bring his resources together and put them into a situation where they must commit to the success of his goals.

XI-36

He must put his organization into a position where the highest level of performance will yield the highest level of individual profit. He creates a situation where the choice between mediocrity and excellence is the same as the choice between loss and gain. He pushes people forward and then burns the bridges behind. In this way, there is no escape from commitment.

XI-37

He leads people up a ladder of higher and higher expectations with promises of greater reward, and when he determines they have reached the level of performance needed for success, he kicks away the ladder so they cannot retreat.

XI-38

In this way, although people do not understand the detail of his methods or implications of his movements, when the executive asks them to perform, they obey as sheep obey the shepherd.

XI-39

Do not depend upon those who are unwilling to meet the challenge of competitive actions. Those who are unaware of how to adapt to opportunities and obstacles are not competent to command an organization. Those who do not employ appropriate flexibility cannot take advantage of their competitor's weakness nor react to changing circumstances. Those who are ignorant of how to maneuver when surprised by the unexpected are unlikely to overcome threats or seize advantages.

XI-40

When a skilled executive moves into a competitor's territory, he imposes his will. He does not allow his competitor to find reinforcements; he does not allow his competitor to rely on others for support.

XI-41

A skilled executive does not rely on folk wisdom or rumor. He worries only about finding the truth. Accurate, timely, relevant information is his only concern.

XI-42

When you lead, give people rewards that no one else can give. Make plans that do not follow precedent. In this way, people will embrace your vision. You will command the entire organization as if it were a single individual.

XI-43

Lead by example, not by words. Motivate people with the expectation of personal profit. Do not emphasize the risks involved. Put them in situations where they can choose commitment or loss, nothing else. There is no middle ground, no average performance, no barely acceptable outcome. When worthwhile people face this choice, they find the strength to be victorious.

XI-44

Executing successful operations involves shaping circumstances so they are favorable to your strengths and minimize your weakness. Initially, pretend that you are going along with your opponent's tactics.

XI-45

Make your competitor believe you can be led in the direction he has determined for you. Lull him to sleep. In this way, you can execute your carefully developed maneuvers behind a curtain of deception and surprise.

XI-46

From the moment a competitive engagement begins, maintain strict discipline. Communicate only what needs to be known. Act promptly when authorized to proceed.

XI-47

When your competitor shows his vulnerability, adapt swiftly to take advantage of it. Seize the initiative. Turn the tables. Make him dance in time to your music.

XI-48

Evolve your strategy according to the opportunities presented by your competition. Put yourself in position to gain a decisive advantage.

XI-49

So, begin competitive activities quietly and secretly. When your competitor exposes his weakness, move quickly. In this way, your competitor will not be able to adapt in time. The victory will be yours.

Incendiary Attacks

Sun Tzu said:

There are five objectives for attacks by fire: first, to burn personnel; second, to burn supplies; third, to burn equipment; fourth, to burn weapons; and fifth, to burn transport animals. Matches and material required for building a fire must be on hand before beginning. Fires start best in certain seasons—when the weather is dry and the constellations of the Sieve, the Wall, the Wings, and the Chariot are rising. The force of water can also be used to attack. But using fire is more powerful. Water can only divide or isolate the enemy; fire, on the other hand, can destroy him.

XII

DESTROYING REPUTATION

XII-1

Destroying a competitor's reputation is a particularly devious type of competitive operation. It is, however, extremely effective. There are five areas that can be a focus for attacks on reputation: personal relationships; personal history; individual performance; associates or supporters; and methods of operation.

XII-2

Your competitor must have credible points of vulnerability in one or more areas. These points must then be revealed, magnified, and distorted in order to effectively destroy reputation.

XII-3

Further, the raw material of scandal and the resources needed to spread the word must be at your disposal before you begin.

XII-4

The effectiveness of a campaign to destroy reputation depends on the political and cultural environments at the time. Political and cultural currents must carry the bad news readily in order for the damage to spread widely.

XII-5

The appropriate time to begin a campaign to destroy a competitor's reputation is when he has other difficulties to deal with. This is particularly true when he has problems within his own constituency that have not yet found a convenient scapegoat.

XII-6

In planning the campaign, find out which of the five areas contains more sensitive or vulnerable points and focus your attention there. Adapt your attack to reveal, magnify, and distort these points.

XII-7

The first step is to cause a credibility crisis within your competitor's loyal constituents. This is most effective. Pull his support out from under him. Further, if loyal constituents are shaken by your revelations, then others, who are less loyal or outright opposed, will certainly be influenced. If a crisis of confidence begins immediately, follow up quickly with more aggressive tactics. But, if you cannot cause a crisis among his close constituents right away and your competitor remains calm, do not press your attack vigorously.

XII-8

Rather, let the issues simmer on a low flame. Do as much damage as possible and wait. Delay your attack until weakness in support appears, then increase intensity.

XII-9

Sometimes it is not possible to identify the most appropriate avenue for attack on reputation. If you determine that destroying reputation is your best tactic and the time is right, then begin the attack somewhere and observe his reactions to it. Your competitor may reveal his points of vulnerability to you under the pressure of attack.

XII-10

Attempting to destroy a competitor's reputation is a dangerous business. After you have started a destructive campaign, make sure that you are not caught in the backdraft.

XII-11

After political and cultural currents have flowed in a certain direction for a while, they will more than likely shift. Be prepared to modify your tactics or abandon the campaign if time and current turn against you.

XII-12

All executives must be familiar with the five objectives of a campaign against reputation. Executives should be prepared to defend themselves or attack others in accordance with the strategic situation.

XII-13

Destroying reputation is a method of permanently defeating your competitor. Other methods of operation require significant expenditures of resources; and, even if successful, their results may not be permanent.

Sun Tzu said:

Do not attack your enemy unless you can profit from it. Do not consume resources unless there is a corresponding gain. Do not wage war unless you are in danger. A ruler should not raise an army out of passion or rage. A commander should not attack the enemy out of anger or emotion. Move when it is profitable; stop when it is not. Therefore, an enlightened ruler is very prudent and a great commander is very cautious. By doing this, the state is preserved and its defenses maintained.

XII-14

A destroyed reputation, on the other hand, may cost you nothing more than a few well-placed words. More important, once destroyed, a reputation is difficult to restore.

XII-15

To defeat a competitor and then not be able to benefit from the victory is a misfortune. Competing for the sake of competition alone is a waste of time and effort, besides being an unwarranted risk.

XII-16

Therefore, a skilled executive first weighs the benefits to be gained from winning a competitive engagement. Once he determines it is appropriate to begin, he fights to win.

XII-17

Do not attack unless you can profit from it. Do not use up resources unless there is a corresponding gain. Do not react aggressively unless you are in danger.

XII-18

An executive should not compete out of emotion. He should not attack out of anger. Move when it is profitable; stop when it is not. In time, emotion can return to reason and anger return to calm. But no amount of time can return assets wasted in ill-conceived adventures or opportunities drowned in a flood of passion.

XII-19

Therefore, a skilled executive acts calmly and cautiously. By doing this, his own weaknesses are minimized, his reputation is preserved, and his power remains intact.

Using Spies

Sun Tzu said:

A commander who seeks to win fame and wealth through waging war but is not willing to spend money to gain information about the enemy is unwise. The reason enlightened rulers and competent commanders win victories, achieve outstanding success, and surpass ordinary people is that they have critical information in advance. Reliable intelligence comes only from people who have personal knowledge of the enemy. There are five types of intelligence activities: local intelligence, internal intelligence, counterintelligence, misleading intelligence, and continuing intelligence.

XIII

GATHERING INTELLIGENCE

XIII-1

Investing resources to begin a competitive engagement removes these resources from alternative uses. Money and manpower already committed to one situation cannot be used for another.

XIII-2

Competitive engagements may continue for many years while participants maneuver in order to position themselves for a decisive encounter. The reason skilled executives win victories, achieve outstanding successes, and surpass others is that they have critical information in advance, that is, they know their competitor's objectives, resources, and activities. They understand the minds of targeted constituencies. Further, they win because they confuse the competition about their own intentions and circumstances.

XIII-3
Critical advance information and intelligence is not generated through wishful thinking or speculation. It is not provided by people who study events or interpret data from afar.
Really useful intelligence comes from people on the ground,
those who have firsthand contact and personal experience
with the competition and marketplace.

XIII-4
There are two goals for intelligence activities. The first goal is
to obtain accurate, timely information about the objectives, resources, and activities of your competition. The second is to dis-
seminate appropriately misleading information about your own
objectives, resources, and activities. Information can be obtained
from and disseminated through different channels and by different methods. Available channels and methods can be generally grouped into four categories: common sources, internal
intelligence, counterintelligence, and moles.

XIII-5
By combining elements from these four categories of intelligence, no one can know how your information is obtained or
how it is transmitted. A powerful, but invisible, network is
created. This network is the most precious asset of the skilled
executive.

XIII-6
Common sources of intelligence are those that are easily ac-
cessed in the majority of situations. Common sources include, for instance, trade publications, scientific journals,
sales representatives, advertising, and people you meet at
conventions. Common sources of information are also good
channels for disseminating misleading information to con-

fuse the competition. But use them cautiously. Beware of being misled yourself by rumors and folk wisdom.

XIII-7
Internal intelligence comes from people who actually work with or for the competition or important constituents and who have access to important information. These people are primarily executives and technical experts, but may include clerical staff, particularly in smaller companies with fewer information flow restrictions.

XIII-8
Counterintelligence activities utilize the competition's own agents; that is, people who spy for the competition either inside or outside our own ranks. Once we have identified these people and converted them to our purpose, they become our most valuable agents.

XIII-9
Remember that counterintelligence is used by your competition, too. Some of your informants *are,* without a doubt, counteragents. When you discover a counteragent, *use him.* Provide the competition with misleading information. Counteragents are generally believed without question as long as no one is aware they have been discovered.

XIII-10
Moles are agents on our payroll who are regularly employed by constituents or competitors.

XIII-11
No activity is more closely tied to our success than effectively gathering and disseminating intelligence. No reward should

be greater than that given to those who provide essential information. No operations should be more secret than those related to intelligence.

XIII-12

Effective use of intelligence requires mature judgment and subtle manipulation. Only an executive skilled in the use of people can achieve real success.

XIII-13

The impact of intelligence operations is so pervasive, so encompassing, and so universal that there is no activity where it cannot be profitably utilized.

XIII-14

But intelligence operations must remain secret. If the means employed for gathering and disseminating intelligence are known, all involved are doomed to failure.

XIII-15

It does not matter what type of competitive engagement is planned or whose reputation is to be attacked; it is always necessary to know details about the executives involved, their assistants, their advisors, and even the names of their limo drivers. Informants and agents must provide this kind of information. You must use them.

XIII-16

The most valuable information comes from converting the competition's own agents to our use. Once identified, they should be lured away by any and every means. Give them money, guide them, and protect them. In this way, they become important links in our counterintelligence network.

XIII-17

Counterintelligence is the key. An effective network gives us the ability to judge the value of information provided by other channels.

XIII-18

Counterintelligence allows us to determine how effectively misleading information has been transmitted to the competition.

XIII-19

Counterintelligence allows us to devise effective strategies for recruiting, positioning, and protecting moles. Through counterintelligence, we can discover where and how our intelligence network has been compromised.

XIII-20

A skilled executive must be aware of all aspects related to intelligence activities. He must understand that counterintelligence is the crucial element for success in competitive engagements. He must understand that the reward for counterintelligence work should be extremely generous.

XIII-21

The rise and fall of many executives and organizations is the direct result of the effective use of intelligence. Its importance cannot be ignored.

XIII-22

So, skilled executives employ only the most capable people in their intelligence networks. It is through these people that they are able to gain advancement and profit. Intelligence is the essence and foundation of all competitive success.

SUN TZU'S PRINCIPLES: A SUMMARY

1. Learn to fight
2. Show the way
3. Do it right
4. Know the facts
5. Expect the worst
6. Seize the day
7. Burn the bridges
8. Do it better
9. Pull together
10. Keep them guessing

1. Learn to fight.

Competition in life is inevitable. Further, competition occurs in all areas of life. Sun Tzu advises that we cannot learn too much about how to compete. On the other side of the issue, however, Sun Tzu warns against competition for its own sake.

He notes that using competition simply to enrich oneself or to win without being able to benefit from the victory is risky and costly.

Competition should occur when we have something important to gain or when we are in danger. Further, in competitive situations, we should not allow our emotions to govern our actions. Emotion clouds reason and destroys objectivity, both of which are necessary for continuing competitive success. Loss of emotional control is a major handicap, as well as a damaging weapon in the hands of the competition.

2. Show the way.

Sun Tzu tells us that leadership alone determines success. Leadership is a hot topic for business today. And, of course, it was just as important in ancient China. How might Sun Tzu define leadership? Confucius, who lived at the same time as Sun Tzu, taught a great deal about leadership in his analects. An analysis of Confucian teaching reveals that Confucius believed that effective leadership comes from seven characteristics: Self-discipline, Purpose, Accomplishment, Responsibility, Knowledge, "Laddership," and Example. (Many important leaders throughout ancient and modern history—Alexander, Caesar, Jesus Christ, Lincoln, Grant, Lee, Lawrence, Roosevelt, Patton, Marshall, and others—exhibit these seven characteristics.)

—*Self-discipline* means that a leader tends to live by a set of rules that he determines are appropriate for him and acceptable to his constituents. He does not need external motivation to ensure performance.

—*Purpose* means that a leader works to achieve objectives that are important to his constituents and does not constrain his goals with the narrow focus of strict self-interest.

—*Accomplishment* means that a leader defines results in terms of meeting the needs of his constituents.

—*Responsibility* means that a leader takes ownership of the outcomes of his decisions and actions.

—*Knowledge* means that a leader constantly strives to improve his understanding and ability.

—*Laddership* means that a leader works cooperatively with his constituents to reach agreed-upon objectives.

—*Example* means that a leader shows the way by his own actions.

Sun Tzu also mentions five character flaws that can lead to failure. These are recklessness, timidity, emotionalism, egoism, and overconcern for popularity.

3. Do it right.

All competitive advantage is based on effective execution. Planning is important, but actions are the source of success. Without effective action, planning is a sterile exercise. Modern management theorists believe that a bias for action substantially improves chances for success.

Sun Tzu states that competitive advantage arises from creating favorable opportunities and then acting on these opportunities at the appropriate time. In other words, winners do the right things at the right moment.

But Sun Tzu also reminds us to govern the desire to act with the need for patience. He teaches us that we can be held responsible for putting ourselves in a position where we cannot be defeated, but others must create the opportunity to win. Hence, we must be willing to wait. Just because we know how to win does not mean we can win. Move when it is profitable and stop when it is not.

4. Know the facts.

To achieve success, you must manage information. Information is the lifeblood of business. Sun Tzu says that information, or the lack of it, determines the probability of success. According to him, if sufficient reliable information is available, victory is certain. Sun Tzu teaches that there are two aspects to information management. One aspect is gathering information. The other aspect is giving it out. You gather information to make good decisions. You give out information to misdirect the competition. In either case, you must know the facts, or you will fail.

The best information comes from firsthand experience. Sun Tzu strongly champions the use of agents and informants to gather and transmit firsthand information. This may sound sinister; but, in fact, intelligence operations are both important and necessary. All organizations and individuals engage in intelligence operations to some extent or another. Wise organizations view intelligence operations as critical and invest the resources needed to make them pay off.

Sun Tzu warns us about relying on "folk wisdom." Folk wisdom is the body of unproven assumptions, unwarranted speculation, and generally accepted opinions that is present in any group of people. Great danger lies in not challenging folk wisdom. Reliable facts always precede successful actions.

Most decisions made during competitive activities have an element of uncertainty. We simply cannot know everything. Even so, decisions must be made. Sun Tzu tells us to consider everything and make our decisions by weighing the potential for success. That is, Sun Tzu is telling us to assess the probability of success before acting. Modern managers have access to a number of simple, but powerful, statistical techniques to assist them in quantifying uncertainty related to information. Deming and others have demonstrated that these techniques greatly improve the quality of decisions. Success on the information battlefield depends on knowing how to use and abuse statistics.

5. Expect the worst.

Sun Tzu issues a strong warning. Do not assume the competition will not attack. Rely, instead, on adequate preparation to defeat him. If you seek something that requires you to compete with someone else to obtain it, it is foolish to assume that person or organization is lying dormant. Of course, the competition is going to try to win the battle. Therefore, adequate preparation is necessary.

Sun Tzu issues another warning related to preparation. Do not tackle difficult problems when adequate resources are not available. Even with superior strategy, you will be defeated if you lack resources. According to Sun Tzu, it is not necessary to have the greatest number of men or the most money in order to succeed. What we must do is closely observe the competition and focus our resources on his weak spots. However, do not underestimate the competition. Consider carefully the meaning of his movements and tactics. Expect the worst in order to succeed.

6. Seize the day.

Quick victory is the aim of competitive action. The most important success factor in competition is speed. To win, do things the simple way whenever you can. Simple methods are effective and inexpensive. Try them first. If they do not work, you still have time to try something else. Staying one step ahead of the competition is worth more than any other advantage. When you are ahead, the competition must react.

Speed and innovation are the keys to staying ahead. Do simple things well. Do a lot of simple things very well, and you increase your chances of winning dramatically. This is particularly true if your competition believes that complexity breeds success. More often than not, complexity just breeds more overhead. Strategies that waste time and exhaust resources never work well. When water flows, it avoids the high ground and seeks the low ground. Successful strategies, likewise, avoid difficult methods and seek easy ones.

7. Burn the bridges.

When people are unified in their purpose, no obstacle can stand in their way. Sun Tzu advises the successful leader to place himself and his constituents in situations where they are in danger of failing. When people know they can fail if they do not work together, they will be unified in their purpose and will maintain their commitment to a set of goals and objectives. The successful leader pushes his constituents forward and then burns the bridges behind them.

Motivation and commitment are the keys to leadership. Sun Tzu tells us that people are motivated by the expectation of profit. When you face obstacles and challenges, focus the attention of your constituents on the benefits of success. Do not tell them about the risks involved because this will demotivate them. To capture their attention, give them clearly defined goals and valuable rewards. Treat people well. Train them thoroughly. The success of the organization is built upon the individual success of its members.

8. Do it better.

Sun Tzu says that in war there are only two types of tactics: expected and unexpected. Effective commanders combine expected and unexpected tactics according to the requirements of the situation. But it is unexpected tactics that create the opportunity for victory. Unexpected, or innovative, tactics cannot be defended against in advance. Innovation is the one weapon that makes you invincible. The power of innovation makes victory certain.

Effective innovation is not necessarily complicated or difficult. Successful TQM programs have shown the value of improving operations a little at a time. This goes back to the idea of doing simple things well. A corollary of this idea is to make simple improvements often. A large number of simple improvements can make a significant difference in performance. Those executives who are skillful at encouraging and implementing innovative ideas have infinite resources in a competitive situation.

9. Pull together.

Organization, training, and communication are the foundation of success. If you organize and train your constituents clearly, you will be able to control their actions in competition. If organization and training are vague, people cannot be relied on. They will fail you at the most critical moment. However, when expectations are clear and organization structure is appropriate for their tasks, people will trust their leaders and follow them even under difficult circumstances.

Training is the essential element in getting people to pull together. The cost/benefit trade-off of effective training is huge when combined with appropriate organization and a reward system that does not demotivate people. Even though the benefits are obvious, most of what passes for training in corporate America is a total waste of time and resources. Why? Because it is boring! Training must be interesting in order to be effective.

Good training leads to common understandings and perceptions. Common understandings are essential for clear communication. This is particularly true during the heat of competition, when it is crucial to manage your constituents. Further, effective training builds constituent loyalty. Sun Tzu tells us that we cannot punish people until they feel loyalty to us; that is, until they consider themselves members of our constituent group. He also tells us that if we cannot punish people, we cannot control them.

Effective training keeps your constituents informed and promotes group comfort and stability. People who are comfortable and stable have healthier emotions and sharper minds. Keep your constituents healthy. Save their energy for important matters. Cherish their morale. Use your constituents carefully so they have reserve energy and capacity. In this way, you will be able to take advantage of unexpected opportunities and the leverage provided by innovation.

10. Keep them guessing.

The best competitive strategies have no form. They are so subtle that neither the competition nor your constituents can discern them. If your strategy is a mystery, it cannot be counteracted. As a result, competitors will be forced to react after your strategy is revealed. This gives you a significant advantage. As Sun Tzu says, "What does it matter if a competitor has greater resources? If I control the situation, he cannot use them." With control, victory can be crafted by those with skill. Even if the competition is strong, with control, you can make him lose his will to fight. Focus on your objective. Maintain control by keeping your strategies secret.

To get control, seize something your competitor wants or needs. When your competitor shows a weakness, move rapidly, without warning. Succeeding in a direct attack depends mainly on deception. The less a competitor knows about where you intend to focus your attention, the stronger you are. If he must prepare defenses at many points, because of limited resources, your competitor will be weak everywhere.